Jenny Mosley's Series
Active Assemblies 3

Vicki Johnson

36 assemblies for each week of the school year for teaching the
Social and Emotional Aspects of Learning.

Positive Press

Published in 2012 by:

Positive Press Ltd

28A Gloucester Road

Trowbridge

Wiltshire BA14 0AA

Telephone: 01225 719204

Fax: 01225 712187

E-mail: positivepress@jennymosley.co.uk

Website: www.circle-time.co.uk

Printed by: Heron Press | www.heronpress.co.uk

Forword:

I am really happy to introduce our <u>third</u> active assembly book to you! Assemblies are vital for lighting up the hearts and minds of everyone attending. They need to be riveting, pacey, fun and above all support everyone to strive towards the values governing the vision of the school.

I worked with Vicki and her staff and children over many years – and I noted their journey of embedding emotional, social and spiritual intelligence within their school community. Vicki's own flame of creativity and quirky humour always lit up her relationships and these assemblies reflect this. All schools need simple but challenging assemblies to set the ethos.

This wonderful book of assemblies does exactly this for you all. Most importantly … they are <u>active</u>! Too much 'preaching' goes on in schools and it turns everyone off. I love the old Chinese axiom: I see and I forget, I hear and I remember, I do – and I understand! The 'doing' element in these assemblies will embed their messages in wonderfully subtle and forever memorable ways. I hope you enjoy their tried and tested ideas. Thank you Vicki!

CONTENTS

Introduction

A wonderful head teacher once confided that there were days when he walked towards the hall at assembly time with no clue as to what he was going to say or do. Nobody would ever have guessed. His assemblies were a delight. They were uplifting, interactive, always pithy, often funny and sometimes unbearably poignant. They were never ever dull, or too long. Most importantly they passed the staffroom test: no one wanted to miss them even for an extra five minute coffee break! For us lesser mortals, here is a potpourri of assembly ideas, all regularly tried and tested, and all presented with minimum fuss and bother. Before you begin, however, it would be good to have;

- an Assembly Box, big enough to be seen from the back of the hall. A cardboard packing case is fine, covered with fabric, wallpaper or paint, the more exciting the better. This becomes the focus for the audience, doubling up as a table or a story box for storing props. It can be draped with material for an instant display, or have posters pinned to its sides. Best of all it can be packed up in seconds to make way for PE or dinner.

- a Lucky Dip cloth bag in which you keep the names of every class on laminated cards or, depending upon the numbers on roll, every child's name stored in class envelopes. Use it to either select a class seemingly at random and choose a volunteer from within the class, or to select an individual name from the school. This way you avoid a sea of hands, or always picking (inadvertently) the same keen volunteer. Your audience will stay alert if they think it could be THEM! This of course can be rigged...you're the adult!

- a microphone for shy speakers, OR a pretend one. Either is good.

You may wish to consider;

- the attention span of the youngest child. How comfortable is it to sit still on the floor for anything longer than 10 minutes? What can be seen from _their_ angle? I know! Depressing isn't it!

- your kind, adult audience who can give you useful feedback on what worked well.

- ensuring everyone has a termly plan of assembly themes, allowing for class follow-up work in Circle Time or PSHE.

- using music to match the mood and to act as cues; the same piece of music for a week allows the children to get to know and recognise different composers or genres. Have the name of the piece prominently displayed, then remove it before using it as a quiz question on the last day. Christmas cracker 'innards' make good prizes, by the way. Pass the time waiting for the inevitable latecomers by playing invisible instruments or tapping the rhythm with one finger on a palm.

• giving the week a pattern such as setting the theme on Monday, celebrations on Friday, singalong assemblies to raise energy levels on Thursday, child-led assembly once a fortnight, birthday assemblies once a month (see notes on Timing below).

• resisting the temptation to use assemblies for 'business'.

• starting your own 'rituals' for leavers, visitors, or new entrants with a school song or drum roll (clap hands on knees and then above your head with a 'cymbal crash').

• reviewing assemblies on an annual basis and allowing all members of the school community to contribute including governors.

• inviting as many visiting speakers as are available and suitable BUT be sure to vet them first! The Mexican wave of boredom is a certainty if you allow a kindly and passionate fossil-hunting great uncle to have the floor for more than 5 minutes as I can testify.

• keeping your own record. No one wants to hear 'the one about the naughty puppy' every term for seven years.

Timing

Like comedy, one of the keys to a successful assembly is timing. Avoid chopping up optimum learning time by timetabling assembly at the *beginning* or *end* of natural breaks. My preference is just before morning play.

Story Telling

If possible try *telling*, not reading, a story. Adopt the same sort of manner as you would when telling a friend what you did at the weekend or sharing a joke. In this way you can adapt pretty much any situation to illustrate the aim of the assembly by pretending that the main character is someone you know, or even yourself when you were little. Dorothy Edward's 'My Naughty Little Sister' gets this just right, and if you know these stories off by heart then go ahead; the eye contact and pausing to look 'sadly' at someone will not happen if the book is in the way. Try and include the children as you tell the story.

When I was about the same age as you, Jake, there was a girl in my class who no one ever wanted to sit next to at lunchtime. Can you imagine why that was, Nasseer? Yes. She had the worst table manners in the world. What do you think she did Edward? You're right, she didn't say please or thank you but worse than that. Frankie? You're right, she didn't wash her hands before lunch but far worse than that… Etc

You might find it helpful to begin and end on a positive note such as *I'm so pleased that no one at this school would ever behave like a girl in my school did one day when...* or *Wasn't it a shame that I didn't go to a school like this one where kind friends and teachers could have shown that girl some good manners.*

Finally, it's a good idea to use a prop from the story hidden in your pocket as a finishing ritual, such as *And I've kept this [produce with a flourish] shell/ hanky/ comb/ notebook/teddy to this very day.*

Knitting

(Once you start on a knitting analogy it's hard to know when to stop. Here are at least three assemblies presented as one. Non-knitters need have no fear.)

 Focus

To develop good work habits and aspirations.

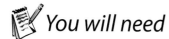 *You will need*

Neat balls of wool and needles, a tangled mess of wool, a piece of knitting that you can easily unravel, if possible, a selection of knitted items such as some baby bootees, a woollen scarf, a tea cosy, a blanket, a jumper, a knitted toy, something big to write on.

 *Opening*

As the children come in begin to cast on, or, if you are a non- knitter, start winding some wool onto a ball; either way look engrossed.

Ask a young child if they know what you are doing.

Who here knows how to knit? (Use the staff as well) *Who taught you? What have you made? Was it easy?*

Bring out the tangled mess of wool.

This is what happened when I first started to knit. I got in a big muddle. And I didn't know what to do about it. What would you have done?

Accept suggestions and ideas such as 'Asked for help', 'Tried again', 'Taken more time', 'Not given up'.

Thank you. Yes, that's exactly what I should have done. Can anyone here remember getting in a muddle when they were learning something new?

(Again, always have a stooge on the staff upon whom you can rely to back up your message).

Take out the easily unravelled piece of knitting (if you have it) to demonstrate how easy it is to undo all your hard work and have to start again.

How do you think I felt when I had to start all over again? You're right! Fed up! BUT just look what happened next!

▶▶ Development

Take an object out of the assembly box and explain what it is. Tell a story about it such as

This blanket is made up of all sorts of colourful squares. Each square was made by friends and then stitched together to make this cosy warm blanket.

Ask for a volunteer to come up and describe another object from the box to the audience. *How does the object feel? What is it for?*

When all the very different objects have been described and admired tell the audience that they were all made *especially* for someone...that they couldn't be bought in a shop...that although they may not be perfect they are all unique. Tell the audience who made which and for whom (make it up if need be) such as

This knitted doll was made by my auntie. She gave it to me for Christmas. These bootees were for my niece. Her granny made them for her for when she was only two days old. Now she's sixteen and she still keeps them to remind her of her granny.

This scarf is rather ragged I'm afraid. It was a present I tried to knit for my dad. It took me ages and I was still learning how to do the stitches but he loved it! Anyone know why?

So what do we need to make a scarf or a jumper like these?

Using the Lucky Dip bag, elicit responses such as wool, needles, a pattern. This might be an opportunity to enlighten some children about what these items are.

And what else?

Yes! Concentration! Patience! Commitment! To be a good counter! '(accept everything especially useful skills).

☁ Reflection

All these things started with just a ball of wool. Everything has to start from somewhere but with these skills (review the list) *just think what you can achieve!*

Top Tips

This assembly might be the start of a whole new school craze. French knitting or finger knitting make good lunchtime activities, as well as crochet and simple knitting clubs, either as after school activities or as part of Golden Time, which might involve the wider community. At one school the children turned finger knitting into ever more elaborate friendship bracelets, and had a competition to make the longest French knitting rope.

Making a Clean Sweep

 Focus

To show that it's always possible to make a fresh start.

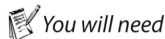 *You will need*

A broom and a bin, the Lucky Dip bag, screwed up pieces of paper left all over the floor with messages on each such as:

To my friend. I feel very guilty because I wasn't nice to you today. I ran off when you wanted to play.

To (name of librarian or whoever is responsible) We left the books in the library all over the floor and no one has picked them up.

To the(name of cleaner) I made a mess in the toilets and I never said anything about it and all the class got in to trouble.

To (name of a class teacher) I didn't finish my work because I was chatting.

To (name of a meals supervisor) I didn't listen to Mrs X at lunchtime.

To (name of class teacher) I pushed Y over in the dinner queue.

(All of these can be related to the Golden Rules if you use them, or adapt them to suit your own school rules. It might be helpful to write which rule applies on the back of the messages)

 *Opening*

This morning I was just about to get out the Assembly Box when I saw there was a horrid mess all over the floor! I'm afraid I haven't had time to tidy it all up. I need help!

Use the Lucky Dip bag to get six OLDER volunteers or at least confident readers.

Thank you, children. Let's get to work. I'll find a broom and a bin. Wait a moment, what's this?

Pick up a piece of paper and ask one of the volunteers to read it out. Look shocked. In turn, the volunteers read out all the messages.

My goodness! Someone wants to get a lot of worries off their chest!

▶▶ Development

Take each message in turn and ask for advice on how the writer should deal with each issue. Use the Lucky Dip Bag. When you hear an excellent suggestion, bring the child to the front and ask her/him to hold the screwed up message.

Recap all the ideas and link them to the Golden Rules or to your school code.

What a relief to get all that sorted! All those worries are so much better out in the open. I think we need to get my bin!

Make a celebration of binning each 'confession'. Such as

Now we know that if we push someone we just need to check that they are alright and that we've said 'sorry'. Next time we need to BE GENTLE!

☁ Reflection

Thank the volunteers and look around for your broom. Use it to sweep the floor as if tidying up from a good clear out.

All those worries are in the bin for today. There will be more, but we can always deal with them, tidy them all away and make a fresh start!

👍 Top Tips

This might be a good way to introduce a Help Box, especially if you have a school mascot of some sort to whom the children can write such as a bear or puppet. The mascot then replies with helpful ideas about how they can resolve their difficulties. At one school the children wrote to Bob the Bear. There was 'Bob notepaper' in each class and a box for his correspondence in a discreet part of the library. He received many letters, all of which had a reply. At the end of the first year it was clear that almost all the letters were from children worried about dealing with change. 'Bob' wrote to the School Council who then suggested that all children had a 'looking forward' week during Y6 visits to High School at the end of the Summer Term, allowing everyone the opportunity to work with staff in whose class they would be for the following year.

Sowing Seeds Part One

 Focus

To foster respect for the natural world and each other.

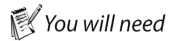 *You will need*

A packet of runner bean seeds and as many other vegetable seed packets as possible, a fresh vegetable which might have been grown from one of the packets, cloak or hat, the Lucky Dip bag.

 *Opening*

I love the story of Jack and the Beanstalk. I'm sure you know it, but let me remind you of the beginning...

Once upon a time there was a boy called Jack who lived with his mother. They were very poor. They didn't have a car or a TV or even a sofa. They didn't have nice warm clothes or shoes without holes. All they had was a little garden and a cow called Buttercup. One day Jack's mother told Jack he would have to sell the cow to buy food. Jack was very sad but he had to do as he was told.

> *What happened next?*

Use the Lucky Dip bag to choose a confident volunteer to be Jack.

Put on the cloak or hat and take the part of the man with the magic beans.

Improvise the next part of the story with the volunteer and make a big deal of the beans.

> *What did your mother think about you coming home with these beans Jack? Yes. I bet she was very cross. And she didn't believe they were magic did she?*

Remove the cloak and step out of role.

 *Development*

But do you know, I think these beans honestly ARE magic.

Hidden inside this bean is enough food to feed everyone in this school! For free! Really! All we need to do is follow the instructions on the packet and we'll get delicious beans.

Look at the other packets and identify the vegetables that will grow from the seeds. Attempt to put a fresh vegetable back in the packet and emphasise how amazing it is to think that such a big thing could come from such a tiny seed.

Take out a bean from the runner bean packet and get the children to guess how much produce might come from one bean seed.

 *Reflection*

That's what I call magic! There are so many magical things in nature...take a moment to be AMAZED!

SOWING A SEED Part two

 Focus

To foster respect for the natural world and each other.

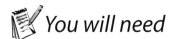 You will need

An A1 envelope with a person drawn on one side (a stick person will do), the Lucky Dip bag, the seed packets from Sowing the Seeds Part One, a flower with petals you can pull apart.

Opening

Remind the children about the seeds that they saw in the previous assembly. Using the Lucky Dip bag find a volunteer to read the instructions on the back of one of the packets. If you have a gardening club, ask the head gardeners to explain what they do to nurture their plants.

⏩ Development

Now pick up the A1 envelope with the drawing on one side.

Aha! A HUMAN BEAN...(sorry I couldn't resist that) But no instructions!

Do you know what we might put on the back of a Human Being packet?

Gather some ideas and write them on the back of the pack.

And I wonder what sort of human being you will grow into? One that's as tall as a runner bean? Or as sweet as a sweet pea? Or as cool as a cucumber?

While you are wondering what sort of adults the children will become take the beautiful flower with which you started the assembly and casually pull it apart, scattering the petals on the floor as you are speaking. Hopefully someone will be shocked by this but if not look down at the tatty remains in surprise. Either way, say,

Oh dear. I've torn this flower. Can anyone put it back together again? Ask for a volunteer.

No? But it took so long to grow!

Reflection

We take an even longer time to grow, longer than the runner beans or the pumpkins here. We need lots of care and attention. When we start our lives we have as much possibility inside us as any one of these beautiful flowers to grow into something a m a z i n g...so mind out for each other and don't crush someone's feelings...

... like I've just crushed that flower.

We've Got Talent

 Focus

Finding out about each other.

 You will need

A collection of shoes you have gathered from the staff which they might use for a hobby or an out of school activity (this works best when there are some unlikely pairings.), the Lucky Dip bag.

 *Opening*

This school is full of surprises! Today we are running a competition to see how well you think you know your teachers. But first let's take a look at these.

From the Assembly Box bring out the shoes and discuss their uses.

Arrange them in a line across the front of the hall where they can be seen by everyone.

▶▶ *Development*

Now we need an expert panel of judges so as always I'll use the Lucky Dip bag.

Call your panel of randomly selected children to stand to one end of the line of shoes and ask for the members of staff to stand at the other. Ensure that there are the same number of children as adults.

Invite your panel to take turns to pair the member of staff with his or her shoe and ask them to give reasons for their choice.

When all the staff have been matched to the footwear ask them to stand beside their ACTUAL footwear.

Hopefully there will be lots of mistakes!

Ask each member of staff to talk briefly about their out of school activity/hobby/shoe choice.

Well! Just imagine that! I never knew Mrs Jones went scuba diving or that Mr Bass was a jazz dancer.

I wonder what other hidden talents there are in this school?

Reflection

Each and every one of us has a talent.

It may be something we all know about.

It may be a secret.

It may be something you are working on right now.

It may be something that even you haven't found out yet about yourself.

But you've got one. And so have you and you and all of us.

Have you spotted it yet?

 Top Tips

An Assembly Talent Show is a wonderful opportunity for children to shine in a safe environment.

Restrict the participants to the oldest classes and have the Talent Show as an annual event so that everyone knows they'll have a go at some point. Limit the time each child can have.

Sports people can be included by demonstrating their particular skills.

Not every child will want to join in, so have a Hobby Day as well during Talent Week, and give each child a table in the hall on which to present themselves.

Allow anything; Barbie doll collections, scout badges, train sets, shell collections, cards, stamps, favourite books, swimming certificates and even small pets.

One particularly keen 10 year old judo player drew some simple holds and photocopied them for anyone visiting her stall. The children spend the day answering questions about their table display to invited visitors.

Include governors and parents of course. Some children, for whatever reason, will claim that they have no outside interests or hobbies; use school achievements for these children. The key thing is to celebrate everyone in some way.

What Is Stopping You?

 ## Focus

To recognise that we are sometimes our own worst enemies.

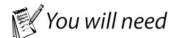 ## You will need

The Lucky Dip bag

 ## Opening

Ask the children to explain what they understand by a reflection, (as in a mirror image).

When you have established a satisfactory explanation, ask for ideas about where one could see a reflection other than in a mirror.

Thank you for those ideas...you may need to remember them when you listen to this story about a very fierce lion.

 ## Development

The Fiercest Lion in the Land

(with optional audience participation)

Allocate sound effects or actions to various groups in the hall either by year group or sections

You will need squeakers, hissers, wavers, tweeters, snappers and one person drawn from the Lucky Dip bag to roar convincingly.

Squeakers, you are going to be rodents. Every time you hear a rodent, of any sort, mentioned in the story, squeak ONCE.

Hissers, you are going to be snakes and so when you hear a snake mentioned in the story please hiss ONCE.

Wavers, you are going to be elephants. Every time you hear an elephant mentioned put up your trunk and wave it in the air. Well Tweeters, please tweet when you hear any type of bird mentioned but only tweet once.

Snappers, please snap your hands together in one loud clap every time you hear a crocodile in the story And finally, Jutvinder, you are the lion. Please roar as loudly as you possibly can.

Are we ready?

Here we go!

Once upon a time there was a ferocious and ruthless creature; his teeth were as sharp as knives, his claws were as deadly as daggers, his eyes were cruel and yellow and his roar made the bravest animal shiver. He was known as the Fiercest <u>Lion</u> (*thank you Jutvinder*) in the Land, or FLL for short.

One sweltering African day, a group of animals gathered at the edge of a wide and beautiful lake.

There were

<u>Elephants</u> spraying the dust from their backs with their trunks full of water.

<u>Water rats</u> (*good listening you rodents*) swimming and playing in the shallows.

<u>Crocodiles</u> lazing in the mud and watching for any <u>water rats</u> that might swim too close and give a lazy <u>crocodile</u> a tasty snack.

There were <u>snakes</u> basking in the heat, and long- legged <u>flamingos</u> who picked their dainty way across the water, ignoring the <u>snakes</u>.

All the animals, the <u>elephants</u>, <u>water rats</u>, <u>crocodiles</u>, <u>snakes</u> and <u>flamingos</u> were content...

until the oldest <u>elephant</u> flapped his huge ears and shuffled his feet.

'I think we'd better go,' he said to his wives. 'I smell danger.'

They sidled away from the watering hole and disappeared into the jungle.

'What's up with them?' little <u>water rat</u> asked his father.

'I'm not sure,' said father <u>water rat</u>, 'but let's not wait to find out,' and he too scurried away with his son not far behind.

'Drat,' said the <u>crocodile</u>. It looks as though the FLL is on the prowl.' He sunk slowly out of sight, like a submarine, leaving a trail of bubbles.

The <u>flamingos</u> turned their heads on their necks and saw that nearly all the other animals had gone. First one then another then all the <u>flamingo</u> flock rose up from the ground and flew far off into the east.

Snake sighed and slithered across the grassy edge of the watering hole and into the safety of the trees.

The lake was still.

The grass shivered and through the leaves crept the <u>lion</u>, his haunches ready to pounce. He was hungry and he could smell dinner.

He stopped and looked around him. There was nothing to be seen apart from the blue clear still lake, steaming in the heat of the day.

He was thirsty as well as hungry and so he padded to the water's edge and crouched down to drink.

But just as he was about to take his first lap with his long rough tongue he looked into the water and saw a ferocious and ruthless creature; his teeth were as sharp as knives, his claws were as deadly as daggers, his eyes were cruel and yellow. The <u>lion</u> *(Well done, Jutvinder)* **leapt back in fear. He had never seen such a ferocious beast before in his life.**

He didn't stop to have a drink, or cool himself in the water, or hunt for the animals that were hiding close by.

He bounded away, his eyes wide with fear and his heart thumping, as far away as he could from the fiercest <u>lion</u> in the land.

Thank you, animals.

Now, what made that lion run away, without even stopping to drink? Yes!

Fear! And what was he frightened of? Yes, himself.

Reflection

Sometimes you might find that the only thing that's stopping you from doing something is YOU! Have you ever thought I can't do that, or that's too hard for me? Who is that 'you' who can't do things, or who won't try things out?

Have a word with yourself! Don't be like the FLL who was afraid of his own reflection, but look yourself in the eye next time you see YOUR reflection and be proud and happy with what you see.

We *all are!*

Something Precious

 Focus

To foster self worth, and to look beyond the superficial.

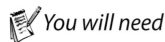 *You will need*

A few exciting looking parcels (shoe boxes would be ideal covered in gold foil. You can make this as complicated or as simple as you like.), a plain parcel without any sparkle in which is a mirror, all covered by a cloth (use ribbon and easily undo-able string, so as to avoid delaying the denouement), the Lucky Dip bag.

 *Opening*

Has anybody heard of William Shakespeare? Can you tell me who he was or what he did? You may be lucky enough to see one of his plays one day. Even though he lived more than 400 years ago, thousands of people still go to the theatre every year to see his plays. This assembly comes from an idea in a play called The Merchant of Venice and as always I will need your help.

Choose enough volunteers to match the number of boxes using the Lucky Dip bag (WARNING: some older children who know you well [!] may be wise to this activity, so you might want to ensure you 'pick' younger or more naive volunteers).

Once the volunteers are gathered, reveal the boxes hidden in the Assembly box. Hopefully you will have put on enough glitter over the <u>gaudy</u> parcels to cause a collective intake of breath.

▶▶ Development

Kind volunteers, today I am feeling very generous and I am offering you, yes YOU, Handa, and you, Jason, and you too (etc) the chance to win a fabulous prize!

Whoever wins the prize of course gets to keep it. And what is more it's the most precious gift anyone can have.

Select your first volunteer to look at all the parcels. Tell her/him to take her/his time and look at all of the parcels with care. I have never ever known a child to choose the boring looking parcel as a first choice, but if they do, it wont matter as you are going to build up the tension by waiting till all the volunteers have chosen a parcel before allowing them, one by one, to un-wrap their parcels. Always start with the gaudiest, and remind each volunteer that they can keep whatever is inside.

Before the boxes are opened ask the volunteer why they chose their box. Make sure you underline the attraction of a sparkly package.

As each box is unwrapped, shake it out on to the floor and say sadly to the volunteer that unfortunately they haven't won the prize today, but give each child a round of applause as a consolation prize.

Pause before opening the last box.

Ask if anyone has heard the expression

'All that glitters is not gold'

Explain that it comes from <u>The Merchant of Venice</u> and ask for some ideas about what it might mean.

When you get to the last sorry looking package, give the impression that you have almost given up hope of finding anything at all.

Make sure the box is opened with care.

What can you see? A mirror, yes. And what is IN the mirror? Take a look. Yes YOUR reflection. The most precious thing in the world...you!

Show the volunteers and allow them to see themselves in the mirror. Exclaim how different and how precious each reflection is.

Hold it up for the audience to see themselves.

Reflection

Sometimes what's on the OUTSIDE (hold up the gaudy paper) gives the wrong impression.

Whatever shape or size you come in, you are a precious gift. ..every single one of you....every single one of us.

This is an adaptation of a Christian Worship Song called:

'Standing in the Need of Prayer'.

There are plenty of free internet downloads of the tune and it works well as an unaccompanied piece with some claps as indicated by **

It's me! It's me! It's up to me!

Let me say it right out loud!**

It's me! It's me! I'm glad to be

Somebody to make me proud.**

-

It's me! It's me! It's up to me!

I can make me feel worthwhile.**

It's me! It's me! I want to be

Someone who will make me smile!**

-

It's me! It's me! It's up to me!

I'm glad that I can make me shine.**

It's me! It's me! I'm glad to be

Somebody I want to call MINE**

Be Good To Yourself

 Focus

To encourage self esteem and healthy habits.

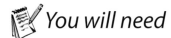 *You will need*

A suitcase (one on wheels) left at the back of the hall for dramatic effect containing your personal items such as: a shopping list for healthy food, toothpaste, soap, flannel etc (or add these to the shopping list), a basic item of clothing, a non-fiction book on any topic, a swimming costume or something to do with physical energy, a photo of someone, a present or thank you card or similar, a pillow and finally, the case needs a large luggage label with ME written on it, folded so that it cannot be read.

 *Opening*

Have you ever heard of a riddle? It's like a puzzle, and usually there's a trick in the question. For example,

What's black and white and red all over?

A newspaper. Do you get it?

Ask someone to explain

Here's another. What gets wetter as it dries? Yes of course! A towel!

If you know a riddle, make a smiley face.

Choose a few examples.

I've got a different sort of riddle, a puzzle about someone. I wonder if you can guess who it is?

There's somebody in this school who needs an awful lot of attention, in fact if I didn't give this person a lot of attention I wouldn't be able to give any to you!

But here's a big clue. This person is older than all of you in Y1,2,3,4,5 and even older than all of you in Y6.

So who, I wonder can it be?

Let's find out.

▶▶ Development

I wonder if someone can bring me that suitcase I left at the back of the hall? I have to have the things in this suitcase all the time for this person who needs so much of my attention. This suitcase has clues inside to help you guess who this person who needs so much of my attention might be.

Bring out the contents and comment on each item, developing those that are most appropriate to your school.

What a long shopping list...fruit, vegetables, milk, rice, fish, eggs, cheese. Well this person certainly needs to eat well.

And look here's a pillow. Yes, I have to make quite sure that this person gets a lot of sleep or there will be trouble in the morning, and I'd never get to school!

I have to keep this person clean to keep germs away and to look as good as possible of course. No one wants to be grubby!

The book is another clue. This person needs to learn new things.

Aha! A swimming-costume. What does this mean do you think?

And here's a very nice thank you card; this person needs to feel appreciated obviously and cared for too by other people like this one in the photograph. So it's not just me who needs to give this person a lot of attention.

Who can it be who needs all my attention before I can give any to anyone else? Who needs to (recap)

- *eat well*

- *sleep well*

- *keep clean and stay healthy*

- *get lots of exercise*

- *learn new things*

- *have friends and feel loved and appreciated?*

Anyone know? Luckily there's a luggage label here.

Look at the luggage label and ask for a volunteer from the audience to come forward and read it out loud, the younger the better. Develop the confusion when the volunteer says 'Me'

*You? Are **you** the person who needs more attention than anyone else in this school? Surely not! Can you read it, Sanjit? Or you, Jayzee? You?*

Let me have a look. Wait a minute! You're right! It says ME.

# Reflection

We need to look after ourselves so we can care for others, be kind to ourselves so we can be kind to others, learn new things and be inspirational to others. Make sure YOUR suitcase has all the things you need to be good to YOU.

Spread the Good News

 Focus

Being positive about each other.

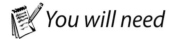 *You will need*

The Lucky Dip bag containing only the names of 6 carefully selected children from across the school who will be confident enough to be able to perform the activity below and who have been briefed about this message in an envelope:

DID YOU KNOW THAT THE PLAYGROUND IS GOING TO BE MADE INTO A LARGE PARK?

 *Opening*

Do you know what a rumour is?

Ask for ideas

Have you ever heard one?

Ask for suggestions

Have you ever heard something that you THOUGHT might be true and told someone else, and then it turned out not to be true at all? A bit like this...

▶▶ *Development*

Bring out your confident volunteers, 'picked' from the Lucky Dip bag.

Have them lined up in a row and spaced so that each child will have to physically walk a few paces to the next.

Introduce the principles of Mix-Up Whispers and explain that each child has to pass on, secretly, whatever they hear to the person next to them. Eliminate all risk of this not going according to plan by briefing your volunteers and giving the **last** child a message you want her/him to say out loud

I've got a letter with some secret information in it for 'A' (the first child in the row). Can you read it and then whisper what it says to 'B' please?

Allow the message to be whispered along the row to each child in turn till it reaches the last child who has been briefed with what to say. Ask her/him to repeat what s/he has heard:

THE PLAYGROUND IS GOING TO BE MADE INTO A CAR PARK

A car park?

Act incredulously and ask for some reaction from the audience. Ask the staff where they think we can play if the playground is to be turned into a car park. Suggest that we'll just have to do without playtimes all together and work an extra hour instead.

Just a second. May I see that message again please, 'A'?

Read out the actual message.

THE PLAYGROUND IS GOING TO BE MADE INTO A **LARGE** PARK

A large park? Now wouldn't that be wonderful news! Imagine! A large park for us all to enjoy together! That's a MUCH better message than the one you thought you had heard isn't it? We started with one thing and ended up with quite another. The volunteers were only playing, but let's try something else.This time we're not going to whisper at all. We're not going to bother with rumours. We're going to say what we want to say out loud and clearly.

Make sure the line is well spread out and stand between 'A' and the child 'B' next to her, to whom you say, for example:

Did you know that 'A' is an excellent actress?

Indicate that the message is to be passed down the line and then ask the last child to walk round to 'A' and say,

I hear you are an excellent actress 'A'!

How does that make you feel 'A'?

Now ask 'C' to say something positive about 'B' and repeat the action all along the line until it gets round to 'B'.

Now how does that make you feel 'B'?

It makes me feel good too when someone says something complimentary about me.

*I'm going to set you all a challenge. I'm going to ask you to spread **good** news about someone, anyone in this school. Look around you now and think SECRETLY who it will be. Don't say anything yet. It might be that they have good manners, or let you go out to play before them, or picked something up for someone. It might be that they are good fun, or a hard worker or kind to their baby brother. Whatever it is that you know is good about that person can you be brave enough to go and tell him or her, or, if not, tell someone else? If you can, do it, and make that person's day! Let's spread the good news about each other out loud.*

Reflection

If you say something complimentary about someone it will make them feel good.

Making them feel good will make you feel good.

And eventually you will hear something good about YOU so you get to feel good twice over.

Top Tips

A school where playground buddies were well established added another layer by making older children into 'undercover guardians'. They were each given a younger child to 'watch out for' and to say something positive to during their first half term in the school. This worked so well that a version was adapted by the PTA who divided up new families between them. Each PTA member made it their business to introduce themselves and say something welcoming to the three or more parents they had been allocated. It was a highly effective way of busting the myth that the PTA were cliquey and encouraged new families to become actively involved.

Finding Friends

 Focus

Getting to know all sorts of people.

 You will need

Some clip boards, paper and pencils, a list of pairs of children with something in common (see below), a photo of your friend, and a prompt sheet for questions such as: What do you like doing? Where do you live? Have you got any pets? What's your favourite TV programme? What do you want to be when you grow up? If you had one wish what would it be? What are you good at?

 *Opening*

I'm going to introduce you to my very best friend.

Show the children your photo and tell them a little bit about the friend. This is a good opportunity to draw them into a story. Make it up or share a real funny incident. Keep it short. Emphasise the good qualities that your friend has and how you've kept friends with each other for so long.

Ask a child who you KNOW will be sensitive to describe someone in his/her class who is a friend without giving a name. Try and encourage a list of qualities rather than a description.

*Well! That could be almost anyone in this hall! If you think you know someone like the person X has been describing cross your arms. If you think **you** are like that person sit up even straighter than before.*

⏭ Development

But look how many possible OTHER friends there are here in this hall... I need some people who can discover some <u>new</u> friends' facts.

Select three or four older children and bring them to the front. Ask them to choose a younger child whom they have never ever spoken to before. Give them the clipboards and, with supervision from a member of staff, ask them to leave the hall and work in pairs to find out as much as possible about the child they have chosen. Warn them that they are going to introduce them to the school in 5 minutes time.

Whilst the friendship fact-finders are busy we are going to make a friendship chain.

OPTION ONE

For this option you will need to know the children well and to have thought up some pairings ready to use. It should be something like this:

Meet Errol from Y5. Bring him to the front. *He has a huge dog who meets him every day from school. But did you know Sylvie in Y1 has a dog too who waits for her at home?*

Bring Sylvie out to the front to stand next to Errol.

Errol, meet Sylvie. Sylvie likes playing ball at playtime. But did you know that Graham in Y6 is good at juggling with balls?

Bring Graham out to the front to stand next to Sylvie.

Sylvie, meet Graham. Graham has school dinner every Wednesday when there's always a roast, but did you know Ayesha in YR loves roast dinner too?

Bring Ayesha out to the front and continue this way until you have a row of contrasting children, preferably a younger and older mix.

Once you've got a line, put them physically together by linking arms.

Children, meet (touch each one on the shoulder as you go down the line and ask each child to repeat their name) *Errol, who has a huge dog who waits for him every day after school....* etc.

OPTION TWO

Use this option if you are less familiar with the children in your school.

Select a volunteer and use a 'microphone' like a TV interviewer thus:

So, can you tell the viewers your name? Jason? Jason, what is your favourite sport/colour/pet/pudding?

Now go to a different class from Jason's and ask if anyone from that class likes the same sport/colour/pet/pudding as Jason. Ask the second volunteer a question and match him or her up to a different child in the same way. Aim to link children together from across the school preferably in boy/ girl, older/younger patterns.

Bring the fact-finders back into the hall and ask them to introduce their partners to the rest of the school.

Reflection

When you go out to play today, look for someone you've never met before and see if you can discover at least three facts about her or him. You might have a surprise!

Top Tips

If you have your break straight after assembly put some fact finder sheets out for the children to use as question prompts.

The 'Have You Met?' board.

A good display/talking point in a public place is to write a description of various children in the school in large captions. Leave out their names as follows:

.... likes football, maths and playing Cat's Cradle. This person wants to be a scientist one day. Have you met?

.... has a baby brother and a gerbil and likes wearing red. This person wants to run a marathon one day. Have you met?

This works well either as a class activity, each class taking a month's slot to feature on the board, or by asking class teachers to supply notes about the children in their classes across the school

What's In The Tin?

 Focus

Don't judge by appearances.

 You will need

Your Assembly Box, the Lucky Dip bag, some books with jacket covers which tell the reader what the book is about, a tin of beans or any tinned food as long as you can read what it says on the label, a tin of fruit with the label removed and a ring pull opener, a large piece of paper with some good qualities written on it that describe a member of staff such as:

Mrs Jones...Patient, fair, won't stand any nonsense, expects the best from everyone...

 Opening

Have you ever heard the expression 'Don't judge a book by its cover'?

I think it's a funny thing to say because I ALWAYS judge a book that way.

Take out the books and (using the Lucky Dip bag) ask for some ideas about what sort of genre the book might be. Read the blurb and draw conclusions with the children about the contents of the book. Make some judgements about the books.

Will I like reading this one? I don't like ghost stories much so no, I don't think I'll bother. What about this one though? Oh yes. Adventure! I'll read this one tonight.

Display the books and then bring out the tin of food with a label.

What's in here do you think?

Go to a young child within easy access and ask for a guess.

Baked beans! Oh goody! I really like baked beans. I'll have that for my supper tonight. It says there's......(read out the contents) so that's OK.

Remind the children that all of the items in front of them are easy to judge. If you like baked beans you'll like this tin of food. If you like reading about trains you'll like this book.

▶▶ Development

But some things aren't as easy. What about this?

Take out the tin with no label. Ask what to do with it. Should you throw it away?

*It could be dog food and I haven't got a dog. **I** certainly don't want to eat dog food!*

Then wonder if that would be a waste. Ask the children for their suggestions using the Lucky Dip bag. When someone suggests that you open it, behave as if you are in quandary.

It might smell nasty! How will I open it without an opener? Suppose it is poisonous.

After a lot of dithering notice the ring pull and very bravely open the tin.

What a surprise! Tinned peaches! I LOVE tinned peaches! They are my very best tinned food! And they smell delicious! Who would have guessed just by looking at that boring old tin what was inside!

Can anyone think of anything else that's hard to judge from the outside?

Accept all suggestions using the Lucky Dip bag until you get to US. (You may need a stooge).

Ask Mrs Jones to come forward.

When I first saw Mrs Jones I didn't know what to expect.

Point out all the differences between you and Mrs Jones such as the way you look, your gender, perhaps, where you live, she likes cats and you like dogs, she's a vegetarian and you aren't etc.

She didn't have a label like a tin of beans or a book jacket. I had to wait and find out. I listened to what she had to say, and saw what she did. I watched her working with you, Class 5, and I heard what you thought about her. And at last I came up with THIS.

Pin the label on Mrs Jones and read out what it says (lots of scope for humour here!)

Mrs Jones...Patient, fair, won't stand any nonsense, expects the best from everyone...

Well! She does exactly what it says on the label...and an awful lot more!

☁Reflection

*If Mrs Jones was on sale in a supermarket I'd buy lots and lots once I'd read the label! But we can't go around with labels on so we need to FIND OUT what's on the INSIDE for ourselves. I know **you** are worth it!*

Six Important Words

 Focus

Saying sorry and meaning it.

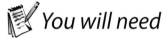 *You will need*

Nothing!

 *Opening*

There are six very important words that I try and remember to use.

'I admit I made a mistake'

Those six words are often the hardest to say. Can anyone think of a good time

to say them?

Collect examples from the audience. It is likely that the children will suggest

mistakes in their work before thinking about mistakes in their behaviour. You

may need to provide some example of your own to illustrate the point.

 *Development*

This story is true...I wonder what you would have done if you were Polly?

Shark Attack

Polly Baker's famous swimming party was at The Oasis. Polly invited her three best friends, Sophie, Anjit and Rory.

Sophie gave Polly some pink nail varnish.

'Wow!' said Polly.

Anjit's present to Sophie was a friendship bracelet.

'I made it myself,' she said shyly.

'It's lovely!' said Polly.

'Open mine now, Polly,' said Rory, handing Polly a patterned box.

Inside was a glittery glass shark, the most beautiful thing Polly had ever seen.

'I chose it for you 'specially from Florida Sea World,' said Rory.

'Very nice I'm sure,' said dad. He wasn't keen on Rory. 'Now then, Polly, give me those presents. You can't take anything apart from a towel into the pool area.'

Polly gave dad her presents, but the box Rory had given her was empty; the precious shark was hidden in her hand.

The noise in the Oasis reminded Polly of the school hall at dinnertime.

Anjit and Sophie jumped screaming into the deep end, but Polly and Rory sat on the side of the pool, dipping their toes into the clammy water and staring at the twinkling shark.

'Do you like it?' asked Rory.

'It's perfect,' said Polly.

She made it zig-zag towards Rory as if it was going to attack. Rory threw up his hands to protect himself, knocking the shark out of her grasp. It fell against the tiles and smashed into a thousand pieces at the bottom of the pool.

They stared horrified into the water where the pieces sparkled and shone like jewels.

'Watch out!' called Polly as a big man waded past them and trod firmly down on to the shards of shattered shark.

'Ow! Help! My foot!' he yelled hopping up and down. 'Something's cut my foot!'

Polly and Rory sat as stiff as statues, gaping as the lifeguards hurried towards them.

'Please leave the pool. There is no need for alarm.'

'Crumbs!' said Rory. 'A real shark attack.'

Polly's dad appeared.

'Sorry, Polly, but the party's over. I've just heard that they'll have to shut the pool. You didn't see anything I suppose?'

Polly and Rory shook their heads, but their hands were sticky with fear.

On Monday everyone was talking about Polly's party.

'My mum says I'm never to go to The Oasis again,' said Dexter. 'She says it's dirty and dangerous.'

'So does my mum,' said Manu.

'They'll have to close it down,' said Harry.

'They already have!' said Anjit. 'There's a sign on the door which says "Closed Until Further Notice".'

'That is so unfair!' said Sophie. 'I was going to have MY party there next month.'

Polly tip-toed away to find Rory.

'I didn't mean The Oasis to close,' said Polly. 'I just thought it would be hard to explain how my shark ended up shattered in the pool.'

They stood for a moment, scuffing their feet.

Then Polly looked at Rory and Rory looked at Polly and they both said together, 'Let's tell.'

Without another word the two sorry children walked back into the school together.

'I can't say it,' said Polly, 'but I could write it.'

Rory nodded.

"Dear Mrs Miller,

We have done something very bad. It is going to make everyone very cross with us but if we don't tell you it will be worse.

Please can you help?

Rory and Polly [Y2]"

They put the letter under the staff room door, and crept away. For the first time since the famous swimming party, Polly felt as though things might, just might get back to normal.

Reflection

Everyone makes mistakes. It's fine. It's always hard to admit them though, and even harder to say sorry and really mean it.

Show me six fingers and let's practice those six words together out loud for the next time we need to use them.'

Top Tips

You may wish to develop the 'Six Important Words' theme into follow up assemblies...

Five Important Words....You Did A Good Job

Four Important Words...Would It Help If?

Three Important Words...If You Please

Two Important Words......Thank You

The Important Word.....Us

Fact and Tact

 Focus

To encourage sensitivity towards each other.

 You will need

An odd outfit: something incongruous rather than comical such as a dressing gown over your normal clothes, a garish scarf, a floppy bow tie, a flamboyant hat, a drum or something that makes a noise, some stooges amongst the staff.

 Opening

As the children come in to the hall let them find you wearing whatever outfit you've chosen. Keep a very straight face and discourage any giggles.

Have you ever heard of a lie detector? It's a machine that the police sometimes use to see if a suspect is lying.

Explain briefly what is involved.

▶▶ Development

Today we are going to be TRUTH detectors. I'll need all of you to listen very hard and I'll need (choose a reliable volunteer) *to listen extra specially hard because X is going to beat this drum every time he hears a FACT and all of you are going to put up your thumbs like so. BUT you must be CERTAIN that it is a fact. You will need proof!*

Are you ready? Then I'll begin.

Today is Monday 4th November (or whatever the date is).

Wait for the beat and if nothing happens explain that was a try out and start again. Otherwise congratulate the children on knowing the date.

Today is Monday 4th November and as it was snowing I came to school on a sleigh.

Wait for a response from the audience.

Nobody? You don't believe me? Why not?

Look for answers from the children but keep it snappy

Exactly! You can see for yourselves that it isn't snowing at all! So that is certainly not a FACT.

I was the first one in to school this morning and so I put the kettle on and made a cup of tea.

Wait for a response.

How do you know? Can you prove it? I MAY have been the first one in or I may not. I may have made myself a cup of tea or I may not.

I put the radio on in my office and heard that... (something topical on the news).

*Just then I saw Mrs Jones and she told me that she was very proud of some children who had ....
........................*

The first child to come to school this morning was ....

I gave her/him 17 chocolate buttons as a reward.

I really like working at this school!

The last statement might be true or not. The children will have opinions about it and will probably say 'I think you like working here' to which of course you can point out that they may think it but they don't KNOW it.

Thank you fact-detectors. Put your thumbs away.

There was ONE fact there which only I can possibly know the answer to...can you think which one it was?

Yes! The last one! I DO like working here, but only I really know that... and if I didn't like working here do you think I would admit it?

Now turn to the staff and go to the first of your stooges.

Mr Brown, I forgot to ask you earlier on but do I look nice in my coat/hat/tie?

Mr Brown: *'Umm yes! Very nice!'*

Thank you! Do you agree, Miss Howard?

Miss Howard: *'Well...oh dear...this is rather tricky...'*

Encourage some tactful suggestions that Miss Howard might try out.

Select the best of the suggestions and praise any examples of tact and kindness.

Take off the item of offensive clothing.

Thank you for your good suggestions. I shan't wear this again in a hurry!

⌦ *Reflection*

Mr Brown and Miss Howard were trying to be tactful. The <u>fact</u> was that I looked silly in what I was wearing didn't I? But they didn't want to hurt my feelings.

Sometimes it's better to say nothing if you think it will make someone else unhappy.

I told a friend his ears were big,

I said his hair looked like a wig,

I laughed because he couldn't spell.

And when he tripped, I laughed as well.

I cannot lie! I can't pretend!

But now

I   haven't   got   a   friend!

Marathon

 Focus

Setting goals for ourselves.

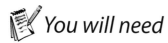 *You will need*

The letters P and B on different cards.

 *Opening*

I wonder if we can work out what the letters P and B might stand for?

Any ideas?

Well it could be lots of things. It could be you, Patrick Bream, or a Pink Bunny or Pretty Badgers even Perfect Boys. Listen to this story and you'll find out.

▶▶ Development

The London Marathon was coming! Sam knew all about it because Sam's dad was running; he'd been training for 6 months. Every night after work, Dad would put on his trainers and track suit and disappear into the night. Every evening in the rain or in the sun, in the dark or light, cold or hot, Dad never missed. Sam missed though: he missed Dad. By the time Dad was back it was too late to do anything except go to bed. On Sundays, Sam and his mum went out in the car and put bottles of water all round the streets where Dad would be running so that he could have a drink on his way.

'Got to keep hydrated,' he explained to Sam.

Sam's mum asked all her friends to sponsor him and she left a sponsor form at Sam's school too to encourage as many people as possible to give money.

'It's for a very good cause,' said Mum.

Two days before the marathon was due to begin all the streets near Sam's house were blocked off with traffic cones. Big tents were put up on the heath where the runners were gathering before the race.

Sam had been in races at school. He knew how to win them and he was fast. He knew that you had to dip as you raced towards the rope at the end of the track to beat the people you were running against. He tried to imagine what it would be like to run for 26 miles. He didn't think he'd ever walked more than 2.

Sunday was Marathon day. Sam's dad had gone before Sam had got up.

'We'll go down to the river and watch the race from there,' said Mum.

By the time they got to the river there was quite a crowd waiting for the runners to pass by. There were people with flags who were waiting to wave, and others with banners saying things like 'Go Dan Go'.

A man on a motorbike drove slowly past them, then a car with a camera mounted on the roof turned the corner and Sam heard people cheering and clapping.

'Here they come,' said Mum.

Around the corner came a runner, pouring water over his head as he ran, his feet barely touching the tarmac. It wasn't Dad. Dad had pink skin and not much hair. This runner was wiry and his skin glistened chestnut brown. The runner let the water bottle fall from his hand as he sped past the crowds chanting and cheering him on.

'Kipchumba! Kipchumba!'

A man next to Sam said to Sam's mum that the Ethiopian runners were the fastest in the world, even faster than the Kenyans.

'Where's Dad?' asked Sam.

Mum didn't hear. The crowd began roaring again as a group of runners pounded towards them, and behind them came more and more until it seemed to Sam as though the street was a bobbing mass of bodies.

'Where's Dad?' asked Sam again. He tugged at his mum's leg. 'Where is he? We must have missed him...'

'What do you mean Sam?' said Sam's mum. 'He won't be here for ages yet.'

'But then how can he win?'

'Win?' said Sam's Mum. 'You didn't think he'd win did you?'

'Well what's the point if he's not going to win?'

Sam began to feel awful for Dad.

The bodies were still jogging past them; thin, fat, tall, short, men, women, young, old, smiling, frowning, waving, grimacing. All of them were being cheered and clapped by the crowd and still no sign of Dad.

A man who looked as if he was riding an ostrich and a team of footballers jogging together went past; men dressed as fairies, ladies dressed as butterflies, superman, Santa Claus, Doctor Who, Humpty Dumpty and still no Dad.

After half an hour they could see the other side of the street again. Empty water bottles and bits of rubbish were left on the road where the runners had been. Now only a few people remained, walking or limping along.

'That's it,' said Mum. 'We must have missed him.'

Sam didn't speak. He felt bad. He knew what it was like to lose a race. He thought of Toby Fowler in Y5 who was always last on Sports Day. It was shaming, embarrassing.

They couldn't get back to the house straight away because of the crowds, and the roads being blocked. They went and had tea with some friends instead. By the time they got home it was nearly four.

The TV was on and there in front if it was Dad.

Sam didn't know what to say to make his Dad feel better. He went up to him to give him a 'never mind' hug. To his amazement his Dad was beaming.

'There you are!' said Sam's Dad. 'Did you see me? Wasn't it great?'

Sam looked amazed. Why was Dad so happy? Had he beaten the Ethiopian runner after all? Had his Dad truly beaten the fastest runner in the world?

'But Dad,' said Sam. 'Did you win then?'

Dad laughed.

'Win? What do you mean? I came 4,505th!'

'4505th? How come you're so happy then?' Sam still didn't get it.

'I beat my PB! My personal best! I beat myself! It was the best time I've ever done and it feels GREAT.'

The Marathon Highlights were on TV, and just at that moment Mum screamed, 'Look! It's Dad! There!'

And sure enough, in amongst the bobbing bodies, Sam could just make out his Dad, smiling and thumping the air with raised hands as he crossed the finishing line, and all three of them jumped around their sitting room cheering and waving at the television again and again and again.

Reflection

So PB means Personal Best, but not just for running. What else might we have PBs for?

Ask for ideas.

Good better best,

Never let it rest,

Until your 'good' is 'better'

And your 'better' is 'best'

Trees Please!

This assembly is a winner, but needs a little preparation.

 Focus

Respect for the natural world.

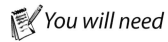 *You will need*

Objects made from trees. Here is a far from exhaustive list to get you started:

Pencils, a book, drawing paper, a magazine and/or newspaper, cards, wrapping paper, wooden toys, an eraser, anything made from rubber, fruits that grow on trees, nuts (if you are allowed to have them in school), a bat, a wooden ball such as the ones used in croquet, or a rubber one, a wooden ornament or decoration, aspirin, spices such as cinnamon, something which symbolises oxygen such as an empty bottle or jam jar labelled fresh air, a picture of a nest or a bird, a picture of a mini beast, something that represents a sun shade such as a tube of sunscreen or sun glasses, wooden furniture, a log for the fire, matches, tooth picks, nail files, wooden spoon, rolling pin, bread board, the Lucky Dip Bag.

Select 20 objects, wrap them in kitchen foil (which is easiest to <u>un</u>wrap) and number them.

You will also need a bag of raffle tickets from 1- 20

As the children come in, give out the parcels to randomly selected children.

 *Opening*

If you have ever had a present given to you in your whole life, put your hands on your head.

Choose a child to answer the following questions using the 'microphone'.

Who gave it to you? What was it? Why did you get a present?

Did you know that everyone here has had hundreds of presents that didn't come from a friend or a member of your family or even Father Christmas? All the presents we are about to unwrap came from ONE THING. Something that lives all around us and that gives us presents every single day of our lives and we're going to find out what it is.

⏩ Development

Ask a child to dip into the raffle ticket bag and pick a number.

Has anyone got a present with this number?

Come down to the front and open the present.

Continue until all the presents have been opened and the children holding the presents are lined up across the front of the hall. Discuss what each object might be and begin to group them into sets following the audiences' suggestions such as 'food', 'cooking things', 'things to play with', 'things to read', 'decorations', 'medicine', 'furniture'.

So who can have possibly given us all these presents? Where have they all come from? What ONE THING is it that gives us fresh air AND apples? A rubber for our spellings AND a doll's bed?

Emphasise the awe and wonder element when **trees** are revealed as the answer.

The medicine is usually a surprise. Extend this with discussions (using the Lucky Dip Bag) on leaf mould, compost, animal habitats and life cycles if there's time.

💭 Relfection

Trees are wonderful. When you go outside, look for a tree and remember what it gives us. Treat them with respect. They have treated you already.

How to feel Rich

 Focus

Feeling good through giving.

 You will need

An old purse, an empty money box, an apple, IOU written on several pieces of paper with space for the amount, the Lucky Dip bag, the Assembly Box.

 *Opening*

I like giving things to people. It makes me feel good. Have any of you given something to someone? A present for your mother perhaps? Or for a friend on their birthday?

Select some volunteers using the Lucky Dip bag and the microphone. Comment on the gifts and the thoughtfulness of the giver. Was the recipient pleased? How did you feel?

Well I'd like to give you all something today because I'm so pleased that you come to our school...and that includes you adults!

Let me see. What have I got here?

Take an apple out of the Assembly Box.

Mr Brown. Would you like this delicious apple for your break? Here we are. I'm so glad you are enjoying it. I'd like to give all of you an apple except that...... there aren't any left. Bother.

I will have to buy some more.

Take out your purse and make a show of finding it empty...and your money box....empty.

I've got no money left! Oh dear and I did want to give you all something except now I come to think there are rather a lot of you (350 or however many on roll) and those apples cost about 10 pence each so that would be? Thank you, Suraj. I certainly haven't got £35:00. So, let me think...

▶▶ Development

What can I give you when I haven't any money? Something that will make you feel good. I know! What about:

A <u>SMILE!</u> (make it a cheesy one and grin all round the hall) That's free!

Or I could give you a <u>hug</u>. (hug a member of staff]).

Or I could give you (point to a worthy child) a <u>well done, thumbs up</u> for working so hard, and you and you and all of Y4 for last week's project etc.

Or perhaps I could give you <u>a laugh</u> (tell a joke). What do you call a one eyed Dinosaur? Doyouthinkhesaurus. And his dog? Doyouthinkhesaurus Rex. No? Can you give me a better one?

Or could I give you <u>a helping hand</u> when you need one?

Or perhaps I could give you some <u>ideas</u>?

Or what about giving you a <u>listening ear</u>?

Or what about giving some <u>time</u>?

Or giving you my <u>attention</u>?

<u>*ALL FREE!*</u>

Can you think of anything else I might give away for free?

Accept everything but look out for friendship, kindness, loyalty, thoughtfulness, help, advice etc.

I've got something here called an I O U. Anyone know what it is? Yes, it's like a promise. I promise to pay you all....A SMILE when I see you (write it in).

And I promise to listen when you need me to (write it in).

This is making me feel very good. I feel RICH now I know I can give you so many things. Anyone else want to make out an IOU?

💭 Reflection

Try giving some things away yourselves. I bet you'll make other people feel better too. We're RICH! Who needs to be a millionaire?

Top Tip

Introduce the children to the idea of Random Acts of Kindness, a movement which is growing across the country. It might be an anonymous note of praise or a jar of flowers left on a desk. I experienced this when I went to my local cafe and found that my espresso had been paid for me by the previous anonymous customer. It requires creativity and imagination, all good!

Let's Face It 1

 Focus

Facing our fears and dealing with them.

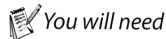 You will need

Some stirring/menacing music; Prokofiev's 'Dance of the Knights' works well, or 'Mars' from Gustav Holst's Planet Suite, a candle, a mask and a cloak, someone to switch on the lights, the Lucky Dip bag.

Opening

The hall needs to be as dark as possible. Make sure the candle is lit before the children come in and sit out of sight by the music source wearing the mask and the cloak.

As the children settle start to play your chosen music, softly at first and then increase the volume. Only you can judge how far to go here. I used to save this for assemblies that didn't include faint-hearted Foundation Stage children.

When the music reaches a climax reveal yourself in the mask and cloak and swirl around for a few minutes.

Give a loud shout, which will hopefully make someone jump, at which point, your accomplice will switch on the lights and turn off the music.

Development

Take off the mask and cloak and blow out the candle.

Now then what was all that about?

How have I been making you feel?

Use the Lucky Dip bag to elicit some responses.

If you've set the scene well someone will soon admit to feeling scared or even frightened.

What was it do you think that made you feel frightened?

Again accept all answers but usually it will be *'I don't like the dark', 'I didn't know what was going to happen', 'The music was too scary'.*

But as you can see it was all a bit of a trick wasn't it?

Because the lights were off and the curtains were drawn the candle made the hall SEEM more mysterious. But actually it's only all of us here for an assembly the same as every day, just no lights!

And the wonderful music does make your spine tingle (play a little bit more) *but it's only music. You can always turn it down* (turn it down) *or turn it off* (turn it off)*.*

And this cloak and mask are only disguises. Nothing more than bits of material and paper, but made to look scary. Now you know it's me are you still scared?

Your brains are amazing. They can make up all sorts of stories and imagine all sorts of wonderful and sometimes not so wonderful things but often they are all just that, your imagination. I set the scene with these props and your imagination did the rest.

Now I'm going to ask you all to be very, very brave if you think you can be.

Put up your hands and adults too, if you are scared of something, anything at all.

Keep your hands up if you are a little afraid of the dark.

Loud noises?

Monsters under your bed?

When I was little I was scared of **** (anything you like here but the more ridiculous and light hearted the better) *****gorillas hiding in the toilet until my sister explained that gorillas didn't like living indoors and that the toilet would be too small for them to fit in to anyway.*

# Reflection

You've been very brave in admitting your fears. The best way to deal with them is to face them, take a good look and they won't seem so frightening. And remember you are not alone. Lots of people feel the same.

# Top Tip

This assembly will inevitably need some follow-up sessions in class, possibly at an individual level. In my experience just the knowledge that many other children have seemingly irrational anxieties is enough to get children to talk about their own fears.

*Good schools will have a listening structure in place...for more information, visit: www.circle-time.co.uk

Let's Face It 2

 Focus

Facing school related fears.

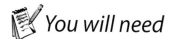 *You will need*

4 paper plates, each with a monster's face drawn on one side and one of the following common fears on the other such as: I'm worried that no one will like me; I'm worried that people will laugh at me; I'm worried that I'll look silly; I'm worried that I won't know what to do, clothes pegs, any book of stories, to be a reasonable actor!

Opening

Have someone peg the faces on your back before the children come in to the hall and stand so that they are hidden.

As the audience settles down look depressed and worried. Give your usual greeting in a very downbeat way. Get out your chosen story book and begin to read with a distinct lack of enthusiasm. Don't let this go on for long before putting down the book, sighing and saying you just can't think about reading a story because:

1. *I've got butterflies in my tummy and I feel a bit sick*

2. *I didn't get any sleep last night*

3. *I can't concentrate on anything.*

Ask the audience if any of them can think what the matter might be? Have any of them ever had those symptoms? Make sure you turn your back to get to the microphone and inevitably someone will call out that you've got something on your back. If they don't, make sure you've planted someone who will!

Development

Ask the person who noticed your 'monsters' to come to the front.

Explain that you can't see what it is so could the volunteer describe what he/she sees.

Look surprised and say that you hadn't realised there were actual monsters pegged to your jumper. Make sure the audience realise that you've been too busy feeling dizzy and headachy to notice.

Ask the volunteer to take one off so that you can see what it is.

Ask the volunteer (if they are old enough) to read out what is written on the back of the face.

'I'm worried that no one will like me'

Look embarrassed and say that you do worry about that, even though you're a grown-up. Say that it's hard to admit to feeling that way but that everyone gets anxious about friendships. Ask if anyone has the same worry. Using the microphone ask the audience for advice. Take the best suggestion and begin to look happier.

I'm not the only one who feels like that then! I feel a bit better. Thank you. Is there anything else on my back?

(Choose the 'worries' that you think most appropriate, but any of the following will be common to adults and children; making mistakes, being laughed at, not knowing where to go or what to do, feeling left out, worried about what other people are thinking or saying etc).

As each plate comes off, stretch your back and look happier. Continue to collect suggestions for dealing with the worries from the audience and keep asking if anyone has the same anxieties. Make sure you show surprise and relief when someone feels the same.

Reflection

*This monster doesn't even **look** like a monster anymore! Nor does this one, or this one!*

Take the first plate and rip it in half.

A trouble shared is a trouble halved.

And if it ever comes back I'm going to take it off, have a good look at it and remember what you said, John, and you, Kwame.

Do the same with the rest of the faces. Make sure you recap on all the good suggestions.

Thank you, children, for reminding me that the best way of dealing with my worries is to face them, and deal with them.

Worrying and doing nothing only makes them worse.

Build a Friend

 Focus

Friendship skills.

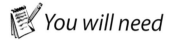*You will need*

A broom stick, a paper plate, Sellotape, felt-tipped pens and scissors, the Lucky Dip bag.

*Opening*

There's a very exciting film I once saw, a true story about a man who survived an airplane crash. He was washed up on an island in the Pacific Ocean, where he was all alone for four years until he at last escaped on a homemade raft. In the film, <u>Castaway</u>, the man makes a friend out of a football because he needs someone to talk to. The ball becomes very important to him. That seems odd doesn't it but put up your hand if you ever talk to

- *your cat*

- *or your dog*

- *your teddy*

- *or a favourite toy.*

Do they talk back?

Encourage a discussion using the Lucky Dip bag.

▶▶ Development

Hopefully, none of us will have to survive on a Pacific island for four years and we'll always have friends around us. But how do we make new friends?

This morning I'm going to try and actually make, I mean MAKE, a new friend from scratch.

Let me see. Well what can I use?

Look along the front row and select some children.

Here's Kayleigh but she's already a good friend. I know because I saw her helping her baby sister.

What about Dan? Hmm, no he's already a good friend because he never, ever bullies others.

I could use Eli but then I know he's good at keeping our golden rules and never gets anyone into trouble so he's already a very good friend.

No, if I want to make a new friend from scratch I'll have to use...aha! this broomstick!

Pick up the broomstick and ask for some suggestions about how to greet someone you don't know.

Apart from saying hello, how are you? Welcome, how do you do? etc, what can I do to make friends?

Look at them and smile? Good idea. Oh dear. The broomstick has no face.

Draw a face on the plate. Emphasise the eyes and ears. Stick the plate onto the handle.

Turn the broom stick away from you and start moaning about how dirty your house is and how the vacuum cleaner has broken and when you get home from work you are going to have to start cleaning and there's no one to help. Stop in the middle of the moan and see that the broomstick isn't even listening to you.

Look at me then! I'm talking to you!

Turn the stick around and start again so that you are facing each other.

That's better! What a good friend this broomstick is! He's listening and listening and hasn't interrupted me once! Thank you, broomstick.

Just a moment. I've had an idea. Could you come home and help me clean the house? You've got good strong bristles and a nice smooth handle. Just the sort of help I need!

⌢ Reflection

You can find your friends in the most unlikely places! My broomstick is just what I need to clean my house, and it certainly never interrupts what I'm saying! If you want to make a REALLY good friend though look for someone who:

- *listens to you*

- *supports and encourages you*

- *doesn't do mean things to other people*

- *keeps the rules.*

Are you that person? Have you got a friend like that already? Cherish that friendship. It's much better than a whole cupboard full of brooms!

Top Tips

Follow on from this assembly with the following PSHE activities for older children:

- ten best ways to make a new friend

- make a guide book to share with the younger children.

- devise a 'good friends' questionnaire and score yourself

- pool ideas for what friendship means in bite sized sentences which can be copied and displayed throughout the school; 'a friend is someone who........'

With younger children use every opportunity to demonstrate how to make and keep a friend. The other adults and I in the classroom were forever pretending to fall out and then demonstrating how to say sorry and make up. If you find this hard, use puppets or stories.

Make new friends but keep the old

One is silver, the other gold!

Emotional Balloons

Focus

Can you guess how I'm feeling?

You will need

A bag of coloured balloons including red, yellow, green and blue, the Lucky Dip bag.

Opening

Take out the balloons and hold up different colours. Talk about the way colours are often used to describe a mood. Using the Lucky Dip bag ask if anyone can help you identify the moods suggested by the colours. Generally green = envy, red = rage, blue = sorrow, yellow = fear, but I've had plenty of other more imaginative suggestions in the past, my favourite being brown for a tummy ache.

▶▶ Development

Suggest how useful it would be if you could carry a balloon to show how you were feeling that day! *Let me show you what I mean.*

Blow up the red balloon.

Who thinks they know how I'm feeling? Chloe? Cross? Yes!

What could you do to help a cross person feel better?

Encourage the children to ask why you're feeling cross. Have some scenarios ready such as

- the car wouldn't start

- I don't feel well but I'm too busy to stay in bed

- I lent a book to my friend and she's lost it.

After a discussion, thank the children for their suggestions, let down the balloon and say you're already feeling better.

Now blow up a blue balloon.

How do you think I'm feeling now?

Repeat the exercise using different volunteers.

Ask if anyone feels brave enough to choose a balloon. Have four very sensible volunteers (who won't be tempted to deflate the balloon too soon for laughs) come up and give each one a red, blue, yellow or green balloon. Explain that you want them to think up an IMAGINARY situation that matches their colour.

While they are thinking, blow up their balloons and ask them to hold them tight without tying them.

▶▶ Development

Do you remember I said how useful it would be if we could show everyone how we are feeling as easily as carrying a balloon?

Now that we know that Jason is feeling sad (blue) we can help him by (collect ideas from the audience):

- *listening to him*

- *supporting him*

- *being a good friend.*

Elicit other suggestions and let down the balloon by degrees until it's deflated.

Repeat with the other balloons until all the balloons are back in the bag.

☁ Reflection

*You see how easy that was? All we needed to know was **how** Jason and the other children were feeling and then we could help.*

But how can we help our friends if we DON'T know how they are feeling?

Yes! Ask them! It's good to talk!

Top Tip

A range of smiley face 'emoticons' found on-line may help younger children identify their feelings and warn others that they need help. Older children may find a colour code useful.

This assembly also works in reverse by starting with an 'in the pink' balloon which gradually deflates as more negativity sets in throughout the story of a particularly tricky day. Ask the children for positive counter actions to inflate the balloon, rather like the 'Good news, bad news' game with the balloon as a barometer.

Heads or Tails

 Focus

To make good choices.

 You will need

A coin, the Lucky Dip bag, 6 cards, each with a forfeit on one side and a number on the other. (Ideas for forfeits might include; bark like a dog, put on a blindfold, feel and identify someone from the audience [member of staff is best] stand on one leg on a chair, sing a solo, pretend to lay an egg, skip with a skipping rope for at least 20 skips).

 *Opening*

Imagine if we couldn't choose anything for ourselves. Imagine if everything we did was chosen for us by the toss of a coin.

Let me show you what I mean.

Use the Lucky Dip bag but choose a confident child from KS2.

Thank you, Sadiq. What have I got in my hand? Yes, a 2p piece. And can you describe for everyone what's on this side? Yes, a head. Of whom? The Queen, Yes. The other side is a little harder to describe. What do you think? Thank you. We're going to call this side 'heads', and that side 'tails'. Thank you, Sadiq.

Now this coin is going to do all thinking for you, Sadiq, but first of all I'm going to ask you if you are prepared to play (dramatic pause!).

HEADS OR TAILS?

Yes? Hoorah! Drum roll for our brave contestant!

Drum rolls are done by simply encouraging everyone to pat their knees in unison and then clap one single clap at your signal.

No shame here for the original volunteer if you have to choose a braver one!

*Let's see what the coin has in store for you, Sadiq. As our brave volunteer I am going to ask you in a moment to carry out some forfeits. If, when I toss the coin, it comes down **heads** up you HAVE to do the forfeit, **tails** up you DONT have to do it. Is that OK? Some of the forfeits might make you look foolish...but we wont laugh at you will we, everyone? They might be things that you might have chosen not to do but the coin is going to make your decisions for you.*

Take out your forfeit cards, numbered on the back. (You must judge what is an appropriate forfeit for your audience).

As you know, whatever you do will be up to the coin. You can't make a decision for yourself, not even which of these forfeits you are going to do. But as the coin can't speak, let me ask (use the Lucky Dip bag) *Matilda to pick a number. 6? Thank you, Matilda. Now, Sadiq, are you good at skipping? How would you like to skip in front of everyone at least 20 times? No stopping or tripping or you'll have to start again! And don't forget, the only thing that can save you is the coin. If it comes down heads you have to skip, tails you don't.*

Give Sadiq at least two turns before asking for another volunteer.

Get the children to talk about how they felt waiting to see what they might have to do.

⏭ Development

Now of course that's just a game, a bit of fun. But think of all the decisions that you make for yourself every day. Who can think of a decision they made before they came to school? What to have on your toast? Which way to walk to school? Whether to pick up some litter in the playground or not? What about if you dropped your ball (it's a good idea to have a ball in your pocket and throw it unexpectedly along the floor) *and it rolled into the road? What would you do about that? What about who to play with at break? HANG ON. What happens when you choose someone to play with? How do you choose? What's involved? What decisions do you make?*

Take the suggestions from the audience having warned them that there are to be NO NAMES and invite children who had an appropriate suggestion to come out to the front. Some will be obvious choices, but hopefully you will have some people who choose to play with someone who looks sad, or is new, or with whom they haven't played before *Look! A moving list! Let's hear those decisions that you made about choosing someone to play with again!*

Where you can, ask the 'chooser' to elaborate.

If need be you may need to start the ball rolling with an example of what you look for when choosing a friend.

Reflection

You are going to have to make hundreds and hundreds of decisions and choices in your life. Some will be little and some will be huge but luckily you won't have to rely on a coin to make the right choice. You will be using your listening skills to hear what others have to say, your looking skills to see what the situation is, your speaking skills to put across your point of view and your thinking skills to make the right choice.

Nuts and Bolts of Friendship

 Focus

Qualities of friendship.

 You will need

A bicycle (not essential but having one will give you more impact), 10 cards, each with a friendship skill (see Development), the microphone.

 *Opening*

Stand up everyone who has a bicycle at home. Stay standing if you can ride it WITH stabilisers. Stay standing if you can ride it WITHOUT stabilisers. Stay standing if you have passed a cycling proficiency test. Congratulations! Stay standing if your name begins with J. All those people still standing please come to the front.

Now, stand up if you have ever been to a swimming pool. Stay standing if you have managed to get into the water. Stay standing if you managed to swim holding on to an adult. Stay standing if you managed to swim with arm bands. Stay standing if you can swim without armbands. Stay standing if you can swim ACROSS the pool. Stay standing if you can swim DOWN the pool. Stay standing if you can swim more than 10 lengths. All those people still standing please come to the front, swimmers to the left and cyclists to the right.

Now we are going to find out how they did it!

Use the microphone to encourage turn taking.

Cyclists, when you cycle, what do you need to do with your feet? Pedal? I see. So when you learnt how to ride I assume you had to practice pedalling.

Get a small group of cyclists to lie on the floor, put their legs in the air and pedal. After a few moments ask them to stop but explain you'll be back to them in a minute.

And of course you will have needed to practise holding onto the handlebars.

Arrange another small group of children to hold imaginary handlebars in front of them and pretend to steer. Again, after a few moments ask them to remember what they did and say you will be back in a moment.

And then there's bell ringing skills.

Get a group to ring imaginary bells and, as before, ask them to stop.

And balancing can be tricky so we'll see how this last group manage by balancing on one leg.

Keep the last group balancing until someone wobbles and once more say you'll be back.

Turn to the swimmers.

And now, swimmers let's see this half do breast stroke with your arms and one leg, and the other half can you do a crawl or a doggy paddle or whatever you can manage with your arms and one leg. You can't use two or you'll fall over!

Is everyone ready? When I give the signal, all of you do your actions as hard as you can.

Marvellous! Look, audience, at the pedalling and balancing and steering going on over there!

Keep up a commentary until the performers have had enough.

⏩ *Development*

Thank you!

Use the microphone and choose an articulate performer.

Is that ACTUALLY how you learnt to cycle Frank?

At this point, gather some stories about how children had help from adults; holding on to the saddle, using the stabilisers, lessons at the swimming pool, swimming with armbands.

If you have a bike, use it to show how none of the cyclists do all these things SEPARATELY, but acknowledge all the skills that are involved none the less.

Can anyone think of any other skills these athletes might need when they are cycling or swimming?

Accept anything but particularly look for learning related skills.

A round of applause for all our athletes please.

Keep 10 children out in the front.

I've got a list here of ten things that you need to be able to do if you want to be able to be someone every bit as important as being a swimmer or a cyclist; someone that we all want and need, someone that we all want to be. Anyone know?

> *A GOOD FRIEND*

In fact these ten things are going to make all the difference to you if you can manage to do them well.

Hand a skill card to each volunteer (You may have your own list here. I've used outcomes from years of successful circle time to suggestion the following top ten).

You will need to be able to:

1. *Share*

2. *Play fairly*

3. *Be helpful*

4. *Be enthusiastic*

5. *Listen*

6. *Be a good loser*

7. *Give and receive compliments*

8. *Say sorry and mean it*

9. *Say how you are feeling...*

10. *... and be sensitive about how others feel.*

Reflection

Riding a bike is tricky and so is swimming but being a good friend is trickier still.

Have another look at this list. Let's get each person to read out their card again. Which of these skills do you think you already do well? Which could you do better? Let's all have a go at (choose a number) *this week and see how we manage. Remember, I'll be watching!*

Top Tips

A friendship board might include 'the skill we are practising this week is....' or you could add it to your newsletter as a weekly reminder, or onto your website.

Sleeping Beauty

 Focus

Gifts we might wish for.

 You will need

Some wrapped presents, suitable for a baby such as baby clothes, a toy or a book, 6 invitation cards (these need be no more than pieces of paper with 'an invitation' written on them), a numbered blank list for each class entitled '**6 gifts to last a lifetime**' , a baby doll wrapped in a blanket.

 *Opening*

As the children come in to the hall, give out the wrapped parcels (making sure the receivers won't fiddle with them) and the 6 cards to any older children.

Recap the story of The Sleeping Beauty as quickly and as snappily as you can.

Don't linger on the gifts that the fairies bring but give a general idea such as the gift of grace, or being able to sing. It may be helpful to use illustrations on the whiteboard or a You Tube version. There are several.

▶▶ *Development*

Imagine that it is this baby's (take out your doll) *party and you are all invited. You've all bought the baby a present. As this is a fairy story it's OK to have an invisible present so Mr Brown, show us what you've bought for the baby. Aha! I see! You are giving the baby a rattle. Can you all show me what you've brought and I'll see if I can guess. Aha, a teddy over there and some clothes here* etc.

Invite the children with actual parcels to come forward and make a show of opening them up and discussing how useful they are to a baby. Make the point that they won't last forever; a baby grows out of a matinee jacket or bootees.

Thank you for the lovely gifts for this baby.

Has anyone else got an invitation to the baby's party?

Introduce the 6 invited guests to the baby's christening and explain that they have magic powers, a bit like the fairies in Sleeping Beauty.

These guests have bought some very special gifts but these gifts are going to last a life time.

Ask the 6 guests for some ideas about what might be worth having. Health? What about beauty? Is it good to be clever? Is kindness a good gift? If possible get the invited fairies to come up with some of their own ideas for gifts or start the ball rolling by asking for help.

We are going to need your help to decide what the gifts might be. Don't forget there are only 6.

Reflection

Be careful what you wish for. Some things that you need might not turn out to be exactly as you thought. This week in your classes talk about what would be the most important gifts to last for a long and happy life. Ooh, happiness! Had you already thought of that I wonder?

Top Tip

Collect up all the ideas on the '**6 gifts to last a lifetime**' lists and make a whole school display. Parents might like to contribute as well.

Put Yourself In My Shoes

 Focus

Encouraging an empathetic response.

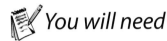 *You will need*

The Assembly Box with a trophy or a medal of some sort, a bandage tied in a sling, an empty chocolate box, a piece of paper or exercise book with a tick and a smiley face, 10/10 or however your school assessments work, the Lucky Dip bag, the microphone.

 *Opening*

Have you ever heard of the expression 'Put yourself in my shoes'? Bear that in mind for a moment as we meet 4 characters.

Using the Lucky Dip bag choose 4 volunteers to sit in front of the audience. Give each child one of the items in the Assembly Box and make sure the volunteer with the sling puts it on the opposite arm to their dominant writing hand.

None of these children know what's going to happen next so let me tell them and you that they are going to be acting. You in the audience are going to help by showing on your faces the expressions that you think these actors should be showing us.

Let me tell you a little about the characters and the situations they find themselves in.

This is Ben. He's got the trophy. He's just been playing football in the five-a-side under 11 football league. His team have just beaten (rival school) Primary School and now they are the best team in the county. May we see your trophy Ben?

Use the microphone and choose a child in the audience to describe how Ben might be feeling.

Well done, Ben. Good acting. A round of applause.

And now for you, Polly. Polly's brother dared her to climb up a tree in the garden. She got near the top and then the branch snapped and she fell down hard onto her left shoulder and now she can't climb anything, or ride her bike or play out or do anything much. Except, of course, luckily her other arm still works O.K. so she can write and do sums.

Use the microphone and choose a child in the audience to describe how Polly might be feeling.

Well done, Polly.

And this is Eli who was really looking forward to this box of chocolates after school except that when he opened them he discovered that his little brother had got there first.

Use the microphone and choose a child in the audience to describe how Eli might be feeling.

Thank you, Eli. Great acting!

And now here's Evie with a very good grade. She was given 10/10 for her spelling test this week and it's the first time she's ever managed it!

Use the microphone and choose a child in the audience to describe how Evie might be feeling.

Well done, all of you actors in the front here and in the audience.

So now we've met the characters, can anyone give me an idea of what putting yourself in someone else's shoes might mean?

 Use the microphone.

▶▶ *Development*

Does anyone here remember Callum Alsop (pick any name)? Callum used to go to this school a long time ago. One day when he was in was in Year 2 he did a very, very brave thing. Let me tell you what it was.

A new boy started in the middle of the winter term. He arrived in the playground at 8:30 and stood waiting to go in to Callum's class. He was thin and shabby and he was wearing tatty trainers even though it was raining.

I'm sorry to tell you that very soon a group of children gathered around him staring. One of the children asked how come he wasn't wearing proper uniform and then another child began to laugh at his trainers and soon all the children were laughing at the new, thin, shabby boy.

Callum felt sad for the boy but it was time to go in to the class and he didn't know what to do. All through literacy he kept thinking about the boy. He could see how miserable he looked and he heard the other children whispering about him. He remembered how his teacher had told them about imagining how it felt to be someone else.

'Put yourself in someone else's shoes,' she had said. 'How would it feel?'

Callum had an idea. He waited until break time and followed the new boy into the cloakroom where all the children were getting ready to go out to play. A gang of children were already laughing and pointing at the new boy.

Callum walked up to him and said loudly and clearly, 'Can I try out one of your running shoes please?'

He took one of the boy's shoes and gave him one of his own, and together the two boys went out to play.

It wasn't till later that the children found out that the new boy's mum had been taken into hospital and that he had had to go into care.

Reflection

What do you think about what Callum did? Would you be brave enough to do the same? Can you think of a time when you made a <u>good</u> difference to the way someone was feeling?

<u>I Make me feel Proud</u>

When I know that something's wrong,

Can I change it, am I strong,

Will I hesitate or dither or delay?

When I see there is a need

To combat somebody's greed

Will I face it, or just turn the other way?

When I hear my inner voice

Say I have no other choice

Even though I do not want to but I ought.

Can I say enough's enough,

Can I make believe I'm tough,

Am I made of stronger metal than I thought?

Can I say out loud

I make me feel proud?

Would I like to be

Someone just like me?

When I say goodbye

Will you think that I

Made a difference to anyone of you?

When the odds are stacked against me

And the writing's on the wall,

When it seems that all my friends have turned from me,

Will I falter, will I alter my belief in what is right

When I know that I am right to disagree?

Can I say out loud

I make me feel proud?

Would I like to be

Someone just like me?

When I say goodbye

Will you think that I

Made a difference to anyone of you?

All Together

 Focus

The value of cooperation.

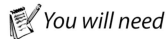 *You will need*

1 large square cut in to 6 pieces, or a smallish jigsaw puzzle, a piece of rope and two buckets, the Lucky Dip bag.

 *Opening*

Before we start, I am looking for three kind volunteers to put this puzzle together for me (use the Lucky Dip bag but with KS2 names only). Have the volunteers put the pieces of the square together, working in front of the audience as you continue with the assembly. Explain that the only rule is they are not allowed to talk to each other and will have to find other means of cooperating and communicating. Also, keep one piece of the puzzle hidden.

Have you ever heard the expression, two heads are better than one? Who knows what it means?

Can you think of a situation that you've been in when you've wished you could have had some help? Use the microphone to collect some stories.

Can you think of a time when you couldn't have managed something on your own?

Let me see if I can explain. Use the Lucky Dip bag and choose two volunteers.

Ask them to sit apart, on the floor, with their legs out straight and their arms folded. Ask a member of staff to time each of them as they attempt to stand up one after the other without putting their arms on the floor.

It's not an easy thing to do is it?

▶ *Development*

This time, try it again but you can sit anywhere you like, and do it at the same time. If the volunteers don't think to sit back to back and use each other straight away (and usually they don't) give them time to try out other ways before asking for ideas from the audience.

Once they have realised that it's easy to stand up when you are using your partner's back for support, let them do it several times to show the audience how much easier things are when we cooperate.

The familiar image of two donkeys tied together with a piece of rope, each straining against the other to attempt to reach two bundles of hay just out of each donkey's reach, is another good analogy for demonstrating working together. Use volunteers to act the donkey parts and take on the role of the farmer, absentmindedly leaving two buckets of food too far apart for the donkeys to reach. Make sure the actors pull apart first or the point will be lost!

Ask the audience for suggestions as to what the donkeys could do to get to their food.

Well done, donkeys.

Together we can do things that we can't manage on our own.

In a good team, everyone has something to offer. Let's have a look at the puzzle.

Ask the three puzzle makers how they've been getting on. Was it difficult? Have they completed it? Do they need more time? What would help?

Produce the missing piece with a flourish.

I've been keeping that piece hidden. Was that helpful? Of course not. I'm sorry, puzzlers. Can you finish the puzzle now?

# Reflection

So what happened when X and Y tried to stand up <u>without</u> using each other for support?

And what happened when the donkeys pulled <u>away</u>?

What about the puzzle? It couldn't have been completed without my cooperation could it?

We achieve so much more when we pull together.

# Top Tips

Have you got a good stock of non competitive games? A quick way to offer lunchtime alternatives to the inevitable football is to teach a new game each week at the end of a PE lesson. Make sure Lunchtime Supervisors are involved. Here are some to get you started:

Mouse Tails

Tuck pieces of string in backs of shoes. Each player tries to tread on the tails in other players' shoes. When a tail is lost, leave it on the floor. Mice without tails can retrieve those that have been left on the floor and continue the game once their tails have been reinstated.

Secret Wizard

All players close their eyes while a wizard is chosen in secret. With open eyes everyone then moves around. The secret wizard casts his spells by running his hand down the backs of the players, who are then frozen. They can only be unfrozen by a hug from another player. The game continues until the wizard is discovered.

Summer playtimes are much enhanced by a stock of donated blankets which children can use for dressing up, picnics, camp, dens or tents and games such as the following:

Peek a who?

Form two teams. Have two people who are not on either of the teams hold a blanket up by the ends so that it is vertical to the ground.

The teams gather on opposite sides of the blanket in a line.

When the blanket is dropped, each player tries to say the person who is at the head of the line's name first. Whoever loses joins the other team. Eventually no one will be left on the losing team.

Who Stole the Cookie?

 Focus

To encourage sensitivity towards others.

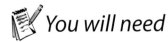 *You will need*

A biscuit tin, a piece of wrapping paper from a biscuit packet put into a member of staff's pocket.

 *Opening*

Make sure the whole school knows the following chant:

Everyone: *Who stole the cookies from the cookie jar?*

Leader: (without missing a beat) *John did.*

John: *Who, me?*

Everyone: *Yes, YOU*

John: *Not me!*

Everyone: *Then who?*

Repeat from the beginning

Who stole the cookies from the cookie jar?

Alison did.

Make sure you keep up a steady beat without gaps between respondents. Continue for a few minutes. Once everyone is nicely warmed up you can add extra claps and hand movements. Have a familiar signal to stop the audience on cue to avoid pandemonium such as raising your hand, calling 'freeze', making a cutting motion, a drum roll and a cymbal clash etc.

So it wasn't Alison and it wasn't John. I wonder who it was?

Bring out at least 4 of the children you had for the chant plus the adult with the wrapping paper in his/her pocket. Please note that the four children need to be carefully selected in view of the activities used for development of this theme.

Today we are all going to be detectives. Somebody here has stolen a cookie from this cookie jar which I keep in my office.

Let's see if we can discover who stole the cookies by the end of this assembly. If you think you have spotted the culprit, raise your thumb at the end of this investigation.

▶▶ *Development*

Take each child in turn and make observations or ask questions about them for example:

What did you have for breakfast, Sanjit?

What time did you get to school?

How did you get here?

Did you pass my office on your way to your classroom?

Make sure you recap on each volunteer's answers with phrases such as,

Aha! So we can conclude then that Sanjit isn't hungry because he had a good breakfast and therefore wouldn't have needed to steal the cookies from the cookie jar! OR

Hmm, Alice walked to school and may have built up a bit of an appetite. Perhaps she wanted something to keep her going till lunchtime.

OR

So John passed my office at approximately 8:30 when I was outside in the playground. Could he have slipped in then, I wonder?

Continue with your sensitive 'interrogation' until you get to the adult. Ask similar questions and act out a little detective work but make sure you mention the meeting you had together in your office before school started at 8:50.

Well, I now need to consider the evidence.

Sanjit wasn't hungry when he got to school and he says he had an apple at break time to keep him going so he had no reason to take a cookie from the jar.

Alice walked to school with her friend, so even though she had porridge for breakfast she might now be hungry again.

And John walked past my office when I was out in the playground and could have slipped in when no one was looking.

Let's look at their faces.

Describe what you see...smiling, serious, thoughtful, innocent, relaxed, nervous...make sure Mr Jones is looking guilty and that the wrapping paper is protruding from his pocket. Keep up the interrogation until a member of the audience indicates that they know 'who dunnit'. Allow the successful detective to come out and show the audience the 'evidence', ie the wrapping paper.

Mr Jones! What have you to say for yourself?

Mr Jones confesses and says that actually he didn't think anyone would mind if he had just one biscuit as he'd missed having his cereal that morning.

But when did Mr Jones have the chance to take a biscuit?

Go over the story and realise that it must have been when he was in the office.

Give Mr Jones the opportunity to demonstrate contrition [!] and allow everyone to return to their seats.

☁Reflection

Poor Mr Jones. He really must have been hungry and I don't mind at all that he wanted to have one of those cookies. Perhaps I should have offered him one straight away. Now I think about it he did look tired and hungry this morning. Oh dear! We don't always take time to notice how other people are feeling. Turn to the person next to you and see if you can detect how they are feeling right now. Can you tell without asking? Look for some clues. Take time to find out. Ask the right questions.

There's usually a reason for people to behave the way that they do.

Whopper Spotter

 Focus

The importance of honesty.

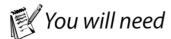 *You will need*

Some watery paint and a piece of absorbent paper or material, three children each with a definition of a word only one of which is right, the microphone.

 *Opening*

'A liar is not believed, even when he tells the truth'

You may know the story of <u>The Boy Who Cried Wolf</u> *or the terrible tale of* <u>Matilda</u> *(who told lies and was burnt to death). If you don't know these stories, ask your teachers to read them to you.*

This morning we're playing Whopper Spotter. I have three children here who have each been given the meaning of a word BUT only one of the meanings is the correct one. Who's telling the whoppers and who's telling the truth?

Make the game as much like a quiz show as possible with the children sitting in a row with their cards. You might want a bell or similar. Act as if you are a games show host thus:

Welcome, everyone, to our ever popular game of WHOPPER SPOTTER. Today we have three contestants eager to slip their whoppers past you. We have one word and three definitions, only ONE of which is the right one. So let's begin.

(Any unusual word plus definitions will do but here's one ready made example)

Distaff

1. distaff is a long straight stick used on important state occasions in Parliament

2. distaff describes anyone on the female side of a family

3. distaff is an argument which occurs between members of opposing teams

Take some questions and then reveal the true definition (2)

▶▶ Development

Of course that was just a game, and I'd asked two people to tell whoppers. But why else might someone lie?

Use the microphone. As you get some good answers, ask those people to stand at the front to make a living list. You are looking for any or all of the following but as always accept everything:

to keep out of trouble

to feel important

to impress friends

to avoid doing something.

Thank you for those ideas. Let's put a story to each of those reasons.

You broke a friend's toy by accidentally standing on it.

She's upset, and wants to know how it happened. You say you don't know

to keep out of trouble.

You told everyone that you and your dad were going to Buckingham Palace to meet the Queen so that you would

feel more important.

You said you were getting a poisonous snake for your birthday

to impress your friends.

You told Mr Jones that you had practised your spellings every day, but that on the day of your test you had a headache so couldn't concentrate which is why you got them all wrong in order

to stay out of trouble.

There's a problem with not being honest though. A lie can grow and spread just like this little blob I'm going to put on this piece of paper. A tiny lie starts small, but soon it spreads and spreads.

Use the watery paint or ink and the material to demonstrate.

Let's take the last example. Mr Jones is so worried about your headaches that he tells me (or the head teacher). I'm so worried I phone up your mum and ask her to come and see me about you. She gets worried that you are in trouble, so you don't dare to admit that you've been telling fibs to get out of learning your spellings. That blob is getting bigger and bigger!

 ## Reflection

Screw up the paper or material.

There's a way to get rid of this lie. Come clean! 'FESS UP! That's about the bravest thing anyone can do!

 ## Top Tip

Have you got an honesty box? Whenever money was found in school the children were asked to hand it in to the school office where it was carefully placed in a small envelope with the finders name and date. Once a month a celebration of their honesty took place in assembly and the amounts that had not been claimed were given back to the finders.

Food for Thought

Focus

This assembly is designed to dramatise the gap between the richest and poorest countries. Please note that though the data dates, the message doesn't!

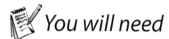 You will need

170 sweets or anything small and edible, bundled into packets of 10, 4 see -through plastic bowls and 4 chairs, a globe or world map would be desirable but not essential, 4 numbered envelopes each with a piece of paper inside which says either citizen of USA, Portugal, Bhutan or Chad.

 Opening

As the children come into the hall, give four confident volunteers (supposedly at random) an envelope.

Imagine if we could get all the food we need to keep us healthy into one useful little pill. Think of it! No more shopping and cooking and washing up. No more arguing about what to eat and how much. No more 'please' and 'thank you' and having to sit at the table till everyone had finished eating. Just pop a pill and that would be that. Although no more tasting delicious fresh strawberries or sucking oranges, licking an ice cream or crunching into a roast potato. Perhaps it's not such a good idea, but, just for this morning, I want you all to imagine that all the goodness you need to keep you alive and healthy for each meal is in this one pill. If you have breakfast, lunch and tea, how many will you need for a day, Y1, and for the week, Y4?

Show the audience the sweets.

*Now is a good time to reinforce your Healthy Eating Policy, should you have one, more of which later!

And now imagine that it's not just you who can manage with one of these pills every day but everyone all over the world; North, South, East, and West, everyone.

Use the globe or map, if you have one, to point out some big continents and ask if anyone can find UK. If appropriate, ask the children to identify other places such as where they went on holiday or where they or members of their family were born.

Now we need to find one of the richest countries in the whole world. Anyone know? Thank you. Step forward the person with envelope number 1, please.

Open your envelope and tell the audience what it says.

So you are a citizen of the United States of America. Welcome to our assembly. Please, take a seat.

Repeat with envelope number 2 and locate Portugal, then Bhutan (South Asia) and Chad (central Africa) welcoming all citizens.

▶▶ Development

Explain that you are now going to give each citizen a bowl of food, apologising to them that it isn't their usual diet.

Tell the audience that what each citizen is about to get represents the amount that the _average_ person in each of these countries has to eat.

Start with the American. Make a big display of counting out 12 bags of 10. Ask the audience to volunteer how many sweets the American has altogether. Split open the bags and pour them all in one bowl together.

Now do the same for the Portuguese citizen who will have 4 bags, and again, ask the audience to calculate how many before pouring them all in together.

When you get to the citizen of Bhutan take out the last bag and say you are very sorry but you only have this amount left. Explain that there are shortages of sweets across the world and that everyone wants to eat so, sadly, the citizen will have to make do with these 7. Open the bag and count out the 7 sweets and pour them into the bowl.

Now one of the very poorest countries in the world is Chad. They can't afford to buy food from other countries and they find it very difficult to grow enough for themselves because of their climate. How many sweets do you think they have to last them a whole week?

Take out the last three sweets and put them in the bowl of the Chad citizen. Look at your Assembly notes...

Oh dear. I've made a mistake. I'm afraid you can only have one.

Give the last two to the American.

☁️ *Reflection*

Say nothing, just look for a moment at the differences between the amounts.

Is that fair? If you hear about something that you think isn't fair you might want to think about what you can do to make a difference. If you think you're too young to make a difference now, remember that one day you won't be, and whilst you're waiting to grow up make sure you remember that we are all citizens, not just of this country, but of the world.

This has the potential to be a very powerful assembly which should raise a great deal of questions. You can vary it by dividing the whole school into continents roughly equal to population sizes and then sharing out food parcels to correspond with the per capita spending on food. When the vast majority of children who find themselves in Africa see what they have to share out between them, and then watch the 10 children from North America enjoying a small pile of sweets each, it usually prompts a fierce reaction.

If your school has a robust Healthy Eating Policy, use this opportunity to throw all the sweets away, but be quick! A European citizen, unable to believe his luck in our sweet- deprived school, crammed the entire week's rations into his mouth before the 'World Health Organisation' could change its mind.

Water

 Focus

To think about the world's resources.

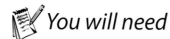 *You will need*

A large plastic bucket of water, a litre bottle of water.

 *Opening*

As the children come into the hall, have KS1 sitting in a semi-circle around the edge of the hall allowing plenty of room for KS2 to sit in the middle.

Imagine for a moment that these children in KS2 represent the whole world's population, not just in the United Kingdom but in every single country of the world.

What do you NEED to have in order to be healthy?

Take ideas from KS2. Stop when you get to clean water. Ask the first 7 children where they get their water from (a tap) but when you get to the 8th say,

I'm afraid there's no water in your home, or even in your village. You will have to walk a kilometre [that's as far as from this school to the motorway or wherever] twice a day and carry all the water that you need for the day, back to your house.

So you'd better get cracking! (You are about to demonstrate that 1 in 8 people world-wide, according to Wateraid, have no access to safe running water. If the 8th child you have picked looks unfit for the following task go along the line until you find a better alternative).

Give the 8th child the bucket and ask him/her to walk around the hall carrying the bucket the best way they can without spilling any water. Ask another child to count how many 'laps' as she/he does it.

Ask the remaining 1 in 8 to stand up, and stay standing, so that we can see how many people are affected.

▶▶ *Development*

Explain that you are going to talk about your day, but that every time you get to an activity that involves water, ask the standing children to turn round on the spot.

So, this morning I got up and had a shower. Then I went downstairs and made myself a nice cup of tea. I fancied an egg for breakfast. I like soldiers with a boiled egg don't you? And then I cleaned my teeth etc.

As you go through your day, make sure the water carrier keeps up the 'toil'.

Have I left anything out?

Gather other examples of water usage.

Now show the litre bottle of water and explain that the average person uses at least 50 of these every day. (Add to the drama by asking for estimates before revealing the actual amount).

How many laps has our water carrier done?

Make a rough and instant judgement about how much further he/she would have to go to reach a kilometre (or set it as a challenge for maths).

Ask the water carrier how he/she is feeling. How would he/she like to do it each day, twice?

☁ *Reflection*

We turn a tap and there's water:

- *for drinking*

- *for cooking*

- *for washing and cleaning*

- *for playing in*

- *for growing our plants*

- *for heating our homes when we're cold*

- *and for cooling us down when we're hot.*

Don't take it for granted...

Pressure Points

 Focus

Making up our own minds and not being swayed by the crowd.

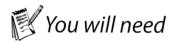 *You will need*

A CD player, a blank CD, any music or talk CD, stooges from either Y6 or the staff, the Lucky Dip bag.

 *Opening*

Make sure the audience know what a CD player does. Show them the CD, the cover and the disc, and discuss where to put the CD in order for it to play. Tell the audience you are looking for excellent listeners. Choose a volunteer to press play and listen to whatever you have chosen for a few moments.

If you heard that piece of music/story/poem clearly please put up your hand.

Thank you.

If you would like me to turn the volume up a little for the next CD please put up your hand.

Thank you.

I'm very pleased with the way that you listened just then. Now we're going to try something else.

▶▶ Development

Take the other blank CD (in a printed cover) and ask for another volunteer.

Explain that the next piece of music is very, very quiet and that you will have to have very good hearing if you want to listen to it.

Ask the children to put up their hands as soon as they can hear something on the CD no matter how quiet it might be.

Ask the volunteer to press play.

Now it's just a matter of waiting. If no one puts up their hand after a minute give a prearranged signal to the stooges to put up their hands. Wait until at least two thirds of the audience have put up their hands, and longer if you can bear it.

Thank you, children.

I'm going to shock some of you now. There was nothing on that CD at all!

Does anyone think they know why they put up their hand?

Accept all explanations until someone is honest enough to admit it was because they saw x had put up *his* hand. Again this eventually will happen. Choose a child who hadn't put up their hand and ask if they were beginning to think they'd made a mistake.

💭 *Reflection*

Ask if anyone can think of a time when they did something, not because it was right, or because they wanted to, but because everyone else was doing it. Don't ask for examples but let the children have a moment silence to think it through.

Let's think for ourselves from now on!

Alone or Lonely?

 Focus

Feeling lonely in a crowd.

 You will need

To have researched the birthdays in Y5, to have some names of good skippers and ball players in the Lucky Dip bag, footballs and skipping ropes, the microphone.

 *Opening*

Some things are best done on your own; reading a book, writing a letter, using the computer or just having a quiet think. Being on your own doesn't mean you're lonely, not at all.

Use the microphone to discover what children like doing by themselves. Make this light hearted and include the staff.

BUT funnily enough, being with LOTS of people can sometimes make you feel very lonely indeed. Let me see if I can show you what I mean.

This part of the assembly needs to feel 'random' but you also need to be sensitive in your choices.

Ask everyone with a birthday in August to stand up. *Stay standing if you are going to be 10 this year, stay standing if your birthday is before the 15th, stay standing if your birthday is after the 7th and so on until there* are no more than three children left standing. (Just one child is fine but s/he will have to be brave!) Make sure they are spaced away from each other.

Now ask everyone to turn away their faces so that no one is looking at the volunteers, just looking towards the front.

Imagine that X, Y and Z have just arrived at our school. They are waiting in the playground to go into their class. They aren't alone are they? Look at all of you here. How can you be alone with 360 children?

All of you sitting down, turn to the person next to you and whisper something in their ears, anything you like, keep whispering until I give you the signal to stop. Make sure X, Y and Z don't hear you.

Use the microphone to gather some suggestions as to how X, Y and Z might be feeling.

Yes, and something else. Everyone has noticed them.

Now, audience, look directly at them. In fact, stare at them as hard as you can without smiling. X, Y and Z, pretend you haven't noticed that 360 children are staring at you and look anywhere but back at them.

Thank you, now STOP. Come out to the front X, Y and Z and receive this round of applause (drum roll/hug) *and let me see the whole school give you a very warm smile. Phew. Are you brave enough to give us some HONEST feedback about how that felt? Did you feel any of these things:*

Foolish? Exposed? Embarrassed? Shy? Anxious? Nervous?

Reassure them that those feelings are what you would expect.

Often, being with lots of people makes you feel lonelier than being on your own.

If your volunteers felt none of the above then praise them for their self confidence.

⏩ Development

So what can you do if you are the one feeling lonely in a crowd?

Use the Lucky Dip bag to select confident skippers and ball players. Choose at least three children.

Sarah is going to show us how good she is at controlling the ball around this little space before passing it to Cody. Michael, can you show us how many skips you can do in a minute?

Allow the three sportspeople to demonstrate for a while, then say 'CUT' like a film director.

Now ask X, Y and Z if there is anything that they have seen that might help them to feel less lonely?

Encourage any suggestions and be prepared for the wildest of answers [!] but the responses to build on will include ideas such as:

Ask to join in, wait for a turn, watch and smile.

Remind the audience how very hard it is to make the first move.

Now I'm going to give you a little tip. It's a good trick. If you want to start a conversation with someone and you don't know how, try this:

You're such a good footballer, Sarah, who taught you?

Do you like skipping, Michael?

Are you in the football team, Cody?

Did anyone notice what I was doing? Yes! I was asking questions!

Demonstrate further by asking questions of members of the audience.

What are you doing this weekend, Sam?

When's your birthday, Millie?

What would you like to play at break today, Tom?

Most people like to be given the chance to say something about themselves, so if you want to make a friend, a good way to start is by asking a question!

Thank all the volunteers and make sure they feel good about themselves and the brave roles they played in the furtherance of PSHE!

⏥Reflection

Being alone is a choice. It's a wonderful skill to feel happy with one's own company.

But feeling lonely can make you sad, it can even stop you doing what you want to do. We can't stop people feeling lonely, but we can make them feel welcome and there's no harm whatsoever in being nice!

Left Out? Right Back In!

Focus

Feeling lonely amongst people you know...this assembly follows on from Alone or Lonely.

You will need

The Lucky Dip bag with the names of confident children, four chairs set out in twos as on a bus, the microphone, a large 'thinks' bubble drawn on a wipe clean board with a sad face, a large 'thinks' bubble drawn on a wipe clean board with a happy face.

Opening

This morning I'm looking for people from the audience who can tell a story but who have no idea how the story will end or even what it's about yet! I need you to be very good at looking and thinking because you are all part of the story. And so, Mr Brown and Mrs Jones, are you!

Invite two members of the staff to join you. Explain that you need two teams of children for some races and that the staff will be the captains. Using the Lucky Dip bag, pull out the 'random' names that you have pre-selected and make sure that there is an even number.

First decide who should go first when picking teams by tossing a coin. Let the staff pick two teams, encouraging them to do it slowly and agonisingly. Whip up some enthusiasm from the audience for each choice. *Hoorah! Good choice!*

Encourage groaning from the opposing team when a favourite choice is taken by the other side. Finally you will be left with just one person.

CUT! Audience. Hands up if this has ever happened to you.

Use the microphone. *How did you feel?*

Return to the 'actor' who was last to be picked.

How do you feel, X?

Why did you leave X to last, Mr Brown?

Is there anything X can think to make him feel better?

Use the microphone and gather some suggestions.

⏩ *Development*

<u>*Somebody*</u> *has to be last, but the last person has still got some choices.*

Here are three. Which do you think would be the best?

1.   *Get angry and walk away*

2.   *Not say anything but feel too upset to play well*

3.   *Decide to make the best of it and play as well as you can.*

Hands up for choice 1...2...3

And now the last person to be picked has chosen choice 3. What can the captain say to make things go well?

Allow all but three of the actors to return to their places.

Remember those choices when we tell you another story.

Sometimes three can be a very tricky number. 'Two's company, three's a crowd'. One person can end up feeling lonely and left out. These three children, X, Y and Z are going to show you what I mean. Don't forget that they have no idea how the story will end, or even what it's about!

Move the actors into positions and encourage them to improvise at appropriate times.

It's the day of the School Trip. A coach has been booked and the whole class are off to spend a day at the Science Museum. X is looking forward to it very much. She is best friends with Y and expects to sit next to her on the coach. But when she gets on she see that Y is sitting next to Z and that she will have to sit on her own.

How do you think she feels?

Use the sad thinks bubbles to record some suggestions such as:

Y likes Z more than me

Y isn't my friend anymore

No one likes me enough to save a place for me

Z is trying to take Y away from me.

Help the audience to see that there are some tricky issues here as there aren't any rows of three. *What can X do?* Use the microphone.

Now use the happy thinks bubble for some positive thinking:

It will make a change to sit with someone else

Perhaps we can swap places on the way back

I need to have a wider circle of friends anyway.

Now finish the story by saying that when they got to the museum X was brave enough to tell Y and Z that she'd felt a bit left out. Allow the actors to improvise a response.

Reflection

It's easy to feel left out.

Don't be afraid to talk about how you are feeling. If you push those feelings away they will keep popping up. X told Y and Z how she felt and they helped her to feel better, but if that hadn't worked, tell someone else.

There are some situations that can't be helped

What you DO about those situations is entirely up to YOU.

Naming and shaming

 Focus

Prejudice and discrimination.

 You will need

A distinguishing feature such as freckles, a mole or birthmark, glasses, different skin colour or anything that you have about which you can do nothing. (If you can't think of anything apply the story to a third person), the Lucky Dip bag, the microphone.

 *Opening*

Before coming in to assembly send a message to each class that you would like the staff to divide the children into those with blue eyes and those with brown. As the children file into the hall, direct the blue eyed children to sit on one side of the hall and those with brown eyes to sit opposite them. Position yourself in the middle of the hall, between the two sides.

Face the brown eyed children predominantly and smile engagingly at them as you speak. Tell the following story about yourself adapting it to sound as plausible as possible.

I'm going to tell you a story that happened to me when I was the same age as you (pick a Y2 child by name).

You may not have noticed but I have lots and lots of freckles/red hair/glasses whatever. My mum used to say that my freckles were sun-kisses OR *my red hair looked like spun gold* OR *my glasses framed my beautiful eyes etc so until this day I'm going to tell you about, I didn't mind at all, in fact I hadn't really thought about it.*

There was a girl called Stella Saunders at my school (choose another name if you already have a Stella). *She and I weren't particularly friends, but I didn't think we were particularly enemies either. But one day, when I was walking in to school, she shouted out 'Hey spotty!' (or 'Oi Ginger Nut' or 'Hello Four Eyes') and then she and some other children laughed.*

It made me feel awful. All that day I felt so bad I couldn't work hard and my teacher was disappointed in me.

When I got home I went upstairs into my bedroom and worried and worried about it. Up until then I'd liked my freckles, but I didn't want to be laughed at over something I couldn't change. The next day I didn't want to go to school and I pretended I had a stomach ache. What should I have done? Brown eyed group, turn to the person next to you and have a few minutes to talk over the problem.

While the brown eyes are talking turn to the blue eyed group and be very fierce with anyone who tries to join in the conversations.

▶▶ Development

Use the Lucky Dip bag and the microphone to gather some suggestions from the brown eyed children.

Thank you. Of course, I should have talked about it to someone I could trust.

In fact, it's not telling tales when someone says unkind things. These things are sometimes too hard to manage on your own.

But why did Stella say such an unkind thing?

Again ask the brown eyed children what they think and allow them to have a few moments to talk it through with a partner. Again, make sure the blue eyed children are not allowed to join in. Use the Lucky Dip bag and the microphone to get to the following suggestions:

She was only teasing

She was jealous

She didn't think I'd mind

She was feeling a bit mean that day and wanted to take it out on someone else.

Those are all good suggestions. The end of the story is that my mum said that my freckles are just part of who I am, and I'm fine with that.

She suggested a good thing to say back if it ever happened again 'I'm perfectly happy with the way I am, actually. I like my freckles.'

As for Stella...well, she and I were never going to be friends but at least she got tired of teasing me as she could see I wasn't going to let it bother me anymore.

Now, all you brown eyed children you are going to have an extra long break

because you all behaved so well.

Wait for the reaction.

What? All of you blue eyed children are so lazy, you'll have to do extra work.

That's fair isn't it?

Using the microphone choose a fair minded child from the brown eyed side to comment. Ask the blue eyed children if they think what's happened was fair.

⌬Reflection

Did you know that in this country it is against the law to treat people differently because of the way they look? No one has the right to make you feel bad for having curly hair or for being tall or short or for having blue or brown eyes. If it ever happens to you, have the courage to tell someone.

Turn to the blue eyed group and smile with unconditional warmth. Ask everyone to stand up and go back to their year groups so that they are no longer segregated.

I played a mean trick and I'm sorry. Now I look at you all I don't see blue eyed children and brown eyed children at all! I see (begin to name some of the children and give them a good quality such as Sensitive Steve and kind Kate etc) *So let's get on with learning together, side by side, no matter what we look like!*

Finish the assembly with an 'Aulde lang syne' type hand shake in time to a favourite song or a conga led by you out into the playground.

Making a Change

Focus

Dealing with change.

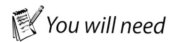
You will need

A box with a mirror in it, two jars of yellow coloured water, a jar of blue coloured water and a jar of red, a clock in view of the audience.

Opening

Before I start, let's make a note of the time. Bill, can you remember that please?

This morning I'm going to make some changes.

First of all, from now on in this school we are all going to- Suggest some foolish changes that you can carry out with a straight face such as:

- all speaking French from now on (demonstrate in whatever language you can manage for as long as you can keep it up)

- our uniform will be pink

- everyone must keep their hands on their heads throughout assembly.

I think I'd better change those changes BACK to how we were, don't you! It's lucky that some changes can be reversed, but there are also some which can't.

Can anyone think of a change that can't be, well, changed?

Take the jars of coloured water and make a big deal of changing the yellow and blue into green.

Make the point that you can't ever change green back to being yellow and blue.

Do the same with the yellow and red colour and make orange.

Express delight with the colours and say they are just what you need for another assembly. Put them aside.

▶▶ Development

And there's something else that changes all the time, slowly but surely, something that can never change back to exactly what it was before.

Get out the box with the mirror inside it and set up an air of mystery and suspense!

That something is in this box.

It's got bigger since we started this assembly! Can you guess what it is?

Use the microphone to gather suggestions. Reveal the contents of the box to someone showing good listening skills and ask them to say what they see.

YES! It's YOU! ME! All of us! Our bodies are getting older all the time and we can't do anything about it, so let's make the best of it.

Invite the oldest Y6 and the youngest YR to step forward and look at the differences in height. Compare their shoes (if they'll allow you to) and ask the Y6 to talk about how they felt when they were in YR, including what they could and couldn't do, what they liked doing then and what they like doing now.

☁Reflection

*What time is it now, Bill? How many minutes have passed since the start of the assembly? You've grown twenty minutes older and there's nothing we can do about that. But think of all the changes that you **can** do something about and make them good ones.*

Making a Change 2

 Focus

Managing inevitable change at the end of a school year.

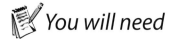 *You will need*

An umbrella, raincoat, rain hat or anything to keep you dry, the paint that you made in 'Making a Change 1', a large sheet of plain paper and two brushes.

 *Opening*

Remind the audience of the changes that were made to the coloured water and how you are now going to use those changes to make more changes! Get out the paper and have it pinned up for everyone to watch as you 'do a Rolf Harris' and paint a field of green grass and a big sunny orange sun. Set the scene for the following story. You may even be able to add an ant and a cricket.

Here's a famous fable that you may know about a lazy cricket and an industrious ant.

It was a hot and dry summer. The cricket lazed around in the fields, singing songs and playing his fiddle. There was plenty of food and nothing he fancied doing other than basking in the sunshine and passing the time very pleasantly. The industrious ant, though, was too busy to enjoy the weather. She knew that pretty soon the summer would be over and that when the winter came she'd need to have plenty of grain stored away. And, of course, by the time the nights were long and the days cold the cricket had nothing to eat and he grew hungry and cold, but the ant had all that she needed to feed herself and her family throughout the winter.

What was the big change that happened in that story? Something that neither the ant nor the grasshopper could do anything about?

What did the cricket do about the change?

And the ant?

Sum up the children's contributions by saying that the ant was, of course, prepared.

⏩ Development

Soon we'll be on our summer holidays. Let's hope the weather will be as lovely as it was in the story of the ant and the cricket! There will be changes though that all of us can expect. What are they?

Take ideas from the audience and bring out the ones that best illustrate the point to make a living list. Make sure they are from all classes as each year group will have different changes ahead.

Reiterate the changes by asking each child to repeat his or her contribution.

What are you doing to prepare yourself for the changes?

Pair up the ideas and suggestions, for example:

Starting a new school

Talk about it with your family and friends

Get all your uniform and equipment ready

Allow yourself to feel excited and anxious. It's what everyone else will be feeling too

Find out who else will be going and arrange to meet with them in the holidays.

💭 Reflection

Even on a sunny day in summer there will be times when the weather will change and there's nothing we can do about it except (take out your rainwear) *be prepared!*

We're proud of the way you've all changed and grown.

We hope you are prepared to face those changes ahead BUT let me tell you something to remember

If you don't like something, change it.

If you can't change it, change the way you deal with it.

 Top Tip

If you have space, add an item on the newsletter with suggestions for families when dealing with foreseeable change at the end of the academic year such as:

Talk about the change; what to expect, what it will mean

Acknowledge any worries or fears no matter how unlikely

Try and involve your child as much as possible in preparation for changes

Ensure that there are some things that remain reassuringly the same even if the child is at 'big school' or in the top class.